SURPRISED BY FAITH

by Dr. Don Bierle

FaithSearch International
105 Peavey Rd., STE 200
Chaska, MN 55318
USA

Surprised by Faith

Copyright ©2003
Donald A. Bierle

ISBN-13 978-0-9745524-9-1
ISBN-10   0-9745524-9-6

Published by *FaithSearch* International
105 Peavey Rd., STE 200
Chaska, MN 55318
U.S.A.

U.S.A. Library of Congress Cataloging-in-Publication Data applied for.

Second edition, revised, August 2006.   9 8 7 6 5 4 3 2

TABLE OF CONTENTS

PREFACE TO THE 2ND EDITION

In a world where change occurs so rapidly that we often stand shaken and in disbelief, it is refreshing and encouraging to find a message that has stability and certainty. It has been eleven years since *Surprised by Faith* was first published. It is astonishing to me that nearly 300,000 copies have been distributed with a likely readership of two to three times that many.

The repeated theme of reader comments is first and often one of surprise to discover the overwhelming body of scientific and historical evidence supporting the truth of the Christian faith. Indeed, during the last ten years the flow of confirming evidence from archaeology for the New Testament text has actually accelerated. Confidence in the New Testament text and the history of Jesus is far greater than when I first wrote *Surprised by Faith*. I have included some of these new discoveries in this second edition.

Another frequent reader response is joyful gratitude upon experiencing the certainty and reality of God in their lives. For many readers, faith had been an illusive and vague concept. God was about religion, they thought, not a personal relationship. *Surprised by Faith* made the familiar yet often overlooked message of God's love, forgiveness of sin and salvation by grace—manifested through the life, death and resurrection of Jesus Christ—to be real. Faith, then, became for them the path to a life-changing relationship with God.

The need for a book such as *Surprised by Faith* has also increased dramatically in the past decade. The flight from confidence in absolutes and a growing biblical illiteracy has left many floundering for any sense of purpose and meaning in their lives. Fear has filled others' hearts as they contemplate the future. I have personally listened to hundreds of people tell their stories of uncertainty and sometimes despair. In *Surprised by Faith* they have found answers that resulted in a God-caused spiritual transformation, and a new life of peace and hope.

The new surprise for me in the past decade has been the acceptance of *Surprised by Faith* across geographical, language and cultural boundaries. The book has been received with enthusiasm among pastors and people in India. Countries around the world have expressed interest as a result of my workshop about it at Amsterdam 2000. Hispanic people have responded positively. *Surprised by Faith* has been translated into Russian, Hindi and Tamil. Several more translations are forthcoming. It is my sense that God has only begun His work of using *Surprised by Faith*—for His glory!

It is my prayer that this second edition will similarly be used by God in the years ahead, to be an oasis for an often disillusioned and spiritually thirsty society—this time on a global scale. But for this to be, I realize more than ever how important it is to embrace the conviction of the apostle Paul: "My message and my preaching were not with wise and persuasive words, but with a demonstration of the Spirit's power, so that your faith might not rest on men's wisdom, but on God's power" (1 Corinthians 2:4-5).

PREFACE

It seems I have always been in school. Twenty-three years of my life have been spent in formal education from the elementary level through two master's degrees and my doctorate. Now, for 30 years and counting, I have been on the other side of the classroom desk as an academic dean and professor. The intellectual stimulation of the academic environment has undoubtedly shaped the development of my thinking. I have always viewed books as wonderfully positive, as treasures to explore. Even in the one-room, rural school I attended for grades one through eight, I read nearly every book our teacher could check out of the town library. Even today I have little sales resistance to the delectable fare served up by publishers' flyers and catalogs that cross my desk.

It also seems I have always thought about God. Growing up in a family that took seriously its Christian heritage, I had considerable exposure to religious instruction. But beyond that, in my private thoughts, I recall often walking along the creek that went through our farm, and wondering "why" about everything from droughts to the death of my pet dog. A hunger for ultimate answers goes back as far as I can remember. My quest for meaning was evident even to the old German minister of our church, and prompted his special visit when I was 14 to encourage my parents to have me prepare for the Christian ministry. At the time, and during the subsequent few years, I did not see "the church" as a source for answers. The field of science had caught my fascination. It satisfied, for a time and to some degree, my inquisitiveness about the world and life.

When you add the attribute of competitiveness to the two ingredients of extensive education and hunger for ultimate answers, you have the formula for an intense search for purpose. This is the background for much of the autobiographical material included in this book. Most of my struggles came during my college and early graduate education. At that time I turned away from what I perceived as the restrictive intellectual climate of traditional religion as I understood it. In its place I found the liberating attitudes of science which I thought held out promise for the fulfillment I was seeking. During this time I mentally either discarded or challenged much of traditional Christian teaching about the Bible, creation, Jesus Christ and salvation. I was asking "why," and could not find the answers. At times I felt there must be something wrong with me since so many people said they "believed" without needing answers.

I now realize there was nothing wrong with my need for answers, and that I was not alone. I was also fortunate. At the height of my search I became acquainted with people who had both asked questions and found answers. For them, intellect was not the enemy of faith. My encounter with them established a reasonable foundation for faith that has reset the direction of my life. Fulfillment had at last come to me.

Many years have passed since then. My understanding of the evidence and reasons in support of the Christian faith has increased significantly. Beginning in the mid-1970s I began to present what I had learned to groups of interested people meeting in private homes. Since then, hundreds of thousands have attended *FaithSearch* events, many who have been quite skeptical, including agnostics and atheists. My goal has been to create a respectful and non-threatening intellectual environment to investigate faith, including the use of logic and scientific evidence. The most frequent comment that I continue to hear from believer and skeptic alike is, "I have never heard of this before! I didn't know there were reasons."

I am writing this book for those who, up to now, have not been as fortunate as I was to find answers. My heart goes out to everyone who cares for truth and the meaning of life but thinks that the Christian faith is intellectually unacceptable. I am also concerned for those who have felt frustrated with the inability to communicate the reasons for their faith in terms that make sense to outsiders. In either case, I believe there is help here.

In the writing of the book I have attempted to integrate two distinct elements: (1) a recounting of my personal intellectual struggles and experiences, and (2) subsequent developments in my understanding through research and mature reflection.

I have tried to make the distinction clear throughout. For example, most of the diagrams in the text were added to clarify some aspect of my earlier struggle. Likewise, the insight gained from some of the biblical stories and illustrations came only after later study and reflection. My purpose in adding both to the book is to give the reader a more complete perspective about faith.

The apostle Peter commanded that believers should "Always be prepared to give an answer to everyone who asks you to give the reason for the hope that you have. But do this with gentleness and respect...." (1 Peter 3:15, NIV). That's what I have tried to do. I hope it will help some to find the path to faith.

"I used my wisdom to test all of this. I was determined to be wise, but it was beyond me. How can anyone discover what life means? It is too deep for us, too hard to understand. But I devoted myself to knowledge and study; I was determined to find wisdom and the answers to my questions...."
Ecclesiastes 7:23-25 (paraphrase)

ACKNOWLEDGEMENTS

This book has been in preparation for many years. Not the manuscript, per se, but the substance has been tested in thousands of lives for over three decades. I am grateful to the students in my college classes whose feedback has been insightful. But it is to the hundreds of thousands who have attended *FaithSearch* events and classes in homes, churches and auditoriums that I dedicate this book. They have questioned, encouraged, dialogued, stimulated, rejoiced, rejected, wept, debated, inspired and otherwise kept my feet on the ground. They are the "flesh and blood" of this book, and my joy.

I want to express deep appreciation to John Eagen for his key role in the development of *FaithSearch* in the early years. Without his initiative at that time, Faith Studies International would not likely have been founded.

Special thanks go to Joel Allen, David Lundstrom and Jake Barnett for reading the manuscript and giving many helpful suggestions. To Jake, especially, I am grateful for his toughness, and for keeping me honest and consistent. I also thank my friend, Nathan Unseth, for his expertise in seeing the manuscript through to publication.

I particularly appreciate the time and encouragement to write that have been given me by the Board of Directors of Faith Studies International. They are always there when I need them, my faithful friends.

Finally, I owe much to God's special gift to me, my wife Vernee. She was an early catalyst in my faith journey, and continues to give unselfishly as we share life and ministry together. In a real sense, she is the unsung coauthor of this book.

Photo Credits

The author extends his heartfelt thanks to the following gracious photographers and/or providers of the photos used by permission in this book.

Page 33: *Magdalen Manuscript*: Used by permission, The President and Fellows of Magdalen College, Oxford

Page 39: *James Bone Box*: Courtesy of Biblical Archaeology Society, Washington, D.C.

Page 40: *Caesarea Stone of Pontius Pilate*: Courtesy of Dr. Boyd Seevers

Page 41: *Capernaum Synagogue*: Courtesy of Jerry Hawkes at www.HolyLandPhotos.org
Inset: Courtesy of Dr. Carl Rasmussen at www.HolyLandPhotos.org

Page 42: *Pool of Siloam*: Courtesy of Dr. Carl Rasmussen at www.HolyLandPhotos.org

Page 58: *Peter's Home*: Courtesy of Dr. Boyd Seevers

Page 61: *Jesus Boat*: Courtesy of Jerry Hawkes at www.HolyLandPhotos.org
Inset: Courtesy of Dr. Carl Rasmussen at www.HolyLandPhotos.org

Page 81: *Temple Mount in Jerusalem*: Courtesy of Dr. Carl Rasmussen at www.HolyLandPhotos.org

Surprised by Faith *"will strengthen your own faith in God, in the reliability of the Bible, and in the truth of Jesus Christ."*
— Dr. Billy Graham

"Simple, concise, and infinitely of value....This book will not disappoint."
— Dr. D. James Kennedy, Coral Ridge Ministries

If you have questions concerning this book, please contact us. The presentation in *Surprised by Faith* is also available in Dr. Bierle's event, *FaithSearch*, a ministry of Faith Studies International. If you would like to schedule a *FaithSearch* in your area, or want information on the audio or video versions, as well as other **FaithSearch** events and resources, please call or write:

FaithSearch
105 Peavey Road, Suite 200
Chaska, MN 55318
United States of America
Phone: (952) 401-4501
E-mail: sbf@faithsearch.org

Book updates and supplemental materials are available online at www.faithsearch.org/SBF-updates.

CHAPTER 1

WHY AM I HERE?

The Crisis of Purpose and Meaning
How to Test Whether God Exists

"Death is the ultimate statistic. One out of one dies."
George Bernard Shaw, dramatist

"The certainty of the existence of a God who would give meaning to life has a far greater attraction than the knowledge that without Him one could do evil without being punished. But there is no choice, and that is where the bitterness begins. Confronted with this evil, confronted with death, man from the very depths of his soul cries out for justice."
Albert Camus (*The Rebel*)

Some might question my right to teach about faith because I have not always thought kindly of it. As an athlete at a Midwestern college, I would enjoy the occasional fun we jocks had mocking the religious types on campus. Later, as a graduate student in biology, I cherished the day that a certain religious magazine arrived in another student's office. That occasion became a special time for us scientists in several disciplines to gather for an exposure of the naiveté of people who wrote in such publications.

PERSONAL CARICATURES OF FAITH

During my undergraduate and early graduate studies in the natural sciences, I was cynical about faith and religious people. I viewed faith as anti-intellectual, an excuse for a lack of hard knowledge. Science, on the other hand, dealt with objective truth in the real world. Religious faith was not truth; it was personal preference and opinion. The strongest faith was that which a believer held on to without real evidence, indeed, in spite of evidence to the contrary!

Furthermore, I caricatured faith as an emotion. It was a kind of security blanket for the less informed and insecure. These people used religion to generate a false confidence. But I suspected that it was an illusion. In reality, I thought, there was little substance there.

It was my third caricature that revealed the most about me. I felt that religious faith was a crutch for weak people. My science associates agreed. It was okay if it helped those who were not able to handle life, but as for me, "I was very successful without it, thank you!"

But this view was not entirely adequate. It was unsatisfying and did not provide answers in my struggle with the significant issues of life. I, like others, struggled with questions and fears concerning death, feelings of personal guilt, and an awareness of an ultimate lack of meaning. Clark Pinnock, a contemporary theologian, has written of what I felt at that time:

> We are experiencing... a loss of meaning in our time... According to humanism, for example, a man or a woman comes into the world devoid of any inherent worth, meaning or direction, entirely on their own. There is no larger purposive order in which their lives participate. There is no significance or value for them which they do not create for themselves. They are driven logically to sympathize with Macbeth: "Life is a tale, told by an idiot, full of sound and fury, signifying nothing."[1]

Why was I on planet earth? What significance and value did my life have? Several years ago the musical sensation, the Beatles, asked a similar question:

> *He's a real nowhere man*
> *Sitting in his nowhere land*
> *Making all his nowhere plans for nobody.*
>
> *Doesn't have a point of view,*
> *Knows not where he's going to—*
> *Isn't he a bit like you and me?"*[2]

12

The Russian novelist, Tolstoy, put it this way: "What is life for? To die? To kill myself at once? No, I am afraid. To wait for death till it comes? I fear that even more. Then I must live. But what for? In order to die? And I could not escape from that circle."[3] It was questions like these that led me to a reexamination of the nature of faith. I came to the realization that my perspective was really a caricature — a cartoon distortion of faith, not the real thing.

> *"The question of the meaning and worth of life never becomes more urgent or more agonizing than when we see the final breath leave a body which a moment before was living."*
>
> Carl Jung, psychologist

THE CRISIS OF PURPOSE AND MEANING

Identifying the Problem: A Finite Orphan

Perhaps an illustration would help at this point. Imagine with me that nothing exists—the entire universe has vanished. We, too, no longer exist. Now let us imagine that some soil appears in this vacuum.

Figure 1.

Some may prefer to call it chemicals or the periodic chart of the elements. To indicate that it's finite, we will put it inside a triangle. What is the purpose of this soil? Every answer to that question assumes the existence of something else. For example, the soil is for growing plants, or as a foundation for trees or buildings. But there are no plants or buildings—only soil. If soil is truly the *only* thing that exists, its purpose cannot be demonstrated.

To solve the soil's problem, visualize grass suddenly appearing on the soil in our imaginary universe. The soil now has a purpose — to grow grass. But what of the grass? In a universe consisting of only dirt and grass, what is the purpose for grass? Some of us would quickly say, "Golf!" But there are no golfers. Others may suggest that it is for food or beauty or to enjoy its softness under foot. But nothing exists

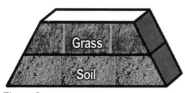

Figure 2.

that eats or looks or can enjoy a walk in its thickness. The grass stands alone with the soil.[4]

Alternatively, grass would find purpose within the context of a universe that includes cows. The grass now exists so that cows can eat and live. But what shall we say for the cows' purpose? To fertilize the grass? To produce milk? But, for what or whom? In a finite world, individual cows may die in order to make room for more cows. However, this suggests that the only purpose of the death of purposeless cows is to make room for more purposeless cows. This is not a satisfying answer and leaves us right where we started. What is the purpose?

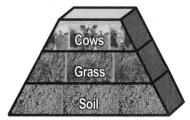

Figure 3.

Part of the problem to this point has been that no rational creatures are present. Only personal beings with rational ability, will and emotion would be concerned with making sense out of this imaginary planet. Dirt, grass and cows do not seek or recognize purpose. What if human beings, capable of rational reflection and having an appreciation of aesthetic values, appeared in the triangle? With humankind now in place, it is all complete. The soil exists so the grass can grow. The grass finds purpose in providing for the cow. And the soil, grass, and cows are there so that humankind has meaning and purpose.

> "Life is just a dirty trick, a short journey from nothingness to nothingness."
>
> Ernest Hemingway, American novelist

But what is that purpose? Why *do* people exist in this imaginary world? In his finite condition and perspective, the best that he can answer is to "dig in the dirt," "mow the grass" and "milk the cow"! Is there nothing more? This is Tolstoy's dilemma: "What is life for? To die?"

Is this imaginary world any different from our own? No! This is our present world of inanimate matter (soil), botanical and zoologi-

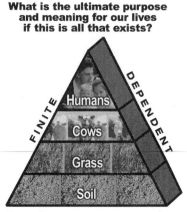

What is the ultimate purpose and meaning for our lives if this is all that exists?

Figure 4.

cal organisms, and humans. The finite triangle is in reality a ball with living things on its surface—the only living things yet detected in the entire universe. Certainly no other intelligent life is known. We are entirely alone in space. If the finite triangle is truly all there is, then all the living beings, including humans, are cosmic orphans. Pinnock points out the problem well:

> Does everyone in fact feel this drive toward meaning...? How is it that there are those who do not seem to ask this question?... Many...have uncomplicated assumptions about meaning and take a great deal for granted. If life has been good to them, they probably have some personal goals—in their job or marriage—which give them enough satisfaction that the question of deeper meaning seems a bit remote. Unfortunately, however, the realities of life have a way of ganging up on a person with shallow assumptions. Something almost always comes along to shatter the dream and raise the issue of meaning for them...which may come in the form of illness or inflation or the loss of a loved one. There are all manner of threats to the meaning of our lives both internal and external which can conspire to destroy it if it is inadequately grounded.[5]

Illustrating the Problem: A Terminal Disease

This lack of a higher purpose and meaning was illustrated to me recently in a conversation with a friend at a class reunion. When I asked him, "What are you doing now?" he responded at some length but in essence said, "I work." I then asked why he was in that type of work and he responded, "Because it pays well." "But why is money so important to you?" I asked. "Because I have to live!" he said as he recounted his house and car payments, educational costs and recreational needs. The acid test came with the question, "Why do you live?" After a pause he glibly quipped, "I guess to work." He had gone full circle: His life consists of going to work and receiving a paycheck which he spends. This requires

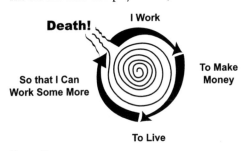

Figure 5.

> "It's not that I'm afraid to die, I just don't want to be there when it happens..."
>
> Woody Allen, film director and comedian

getting up again in the morning to get another paycheck to spend. This will continue until some morning he won't show up for work!

It has never dawned on many that since some morning they will not show up for work their life must be related to some greater reality in order to have any ultimate significance.

If after death my friend could look back upon his life, he would likely ask, "What was the purpose for my life anyway?" As a high school senior and college student, I once was struggling with a decision about vocational choice. I intuitively felt that I wanted my life to count for something. Most of the advice I got was based on economics, where I could make a good living. But I felt that life must ultimately have more value than anticipating a paycheck. Otherwise, in terms of the triangle illustration, I was no better off than the dirt, the grass and the cow. At that time in my young life, I did not know the way out of this dilemma.

CONSTRUCTING A SOLUTION: THE CLAIM THAT GOD EXISTS

It seemed that the only people I knew back then who had some sense of peace about this dilemma were religious ones. Their response was, "Don, God is the answer." They believed their life had eternal value because an infinite and personal God explained where they came from, why they were here, and where they would go after death. But when I asked how they knew there was a God, they would respond that I just needed to believe in Him without questioning. This would only reinforce my view that people of faith and religion were really anti-intellectual. There were no reasons. Evidence, it seemed, had nothing to do with faith.

Wishful Thinking or Objective Reality?

Recently I came across a modern parable that illustrates the struggle I had experienced earlier in my life:

Once upon a time two explorers came upon a clearing in the jungle. In the clearing were growing many flowers and many weeds. One explorer says, "Some gardener must tend this plot." The other disagrees, "There is no gardener." So they pitch their tents and set a watch. No gardener is ever seen. "But perhaps he is an invisible gardener." So they set up a barbed wire fence. They electrify it. They patrol with bloodhounds... But no shrieks ever suggest that some intruder has received a shock. No movements of the wire ever betray an invisible climber. The bloodhounds never give cry. Yet still the believer is not convinced. "But there is a gardener, invisible, insensible to electric shocks, a gardener who comes secretly to look after the garden which he loves." At last the skeptic despairs, "But what remains of your original assertion? Just how does what you call an invisible, intangible, eternally elusive gardener differ from an imaginary gardener or even from no gardener at all?"[6]

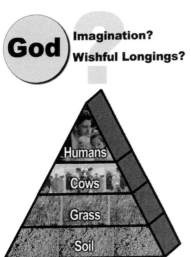

Figure 6.

Obviously, atheist Dr. Anthony Flew wants us to identify the gardener with God and the garden with the world. If God (the circle) is invisible, intangible and eternally elusive from us in the world (the triangle), how can we be sure that God is not just a product of our imagination? If Dr. Flew is right—that there is no God—then we humans would have no ultimate source from which to learn where we came from, why we are here, and what our final destiny is. Said another way, we could not know that our lives have a purpose and meaning that transcends our existence in the finite triangle (from conception to grave). We

"In the form in which men have posed it, the Riddle of the Universe requires a theological answer. Suffering and enjoying, men want to know why they enjoy and to what end they suffer. They see good things and evil things, beautiful things and ugly, and they want to find a reason—a final and absolute reason—why these things should be as they are."
Aldous Huxley,
English author

would be annihilated by death.

But why am I assuming here that we need to have ultimate purpose and meaning? What if life in the triangle is grand and we feel no need for anything more? The answer is that we are only exploring the possibility. It doesn't really matter whether someone feels a need for final purpose and meaning. Rather we should ask, "If there really is an ultimate purpose for us both here and beyond the grave, wouldn't we want to know?" An open mind would want to find out the truth—regardless of whether we felt the need for it—especially if the location of our final destiny were to depend on how we respond in this life.

What we are considering is the possibility that the circle existed before the triangle, and that the circle is infinite and personal—an eternal Being. Of course, an imaginary circle (God) would not help. And just to wish there was a God does not make Him exist. How could we ever know that God is really there, rather than being merely imaginary, created by man's wishful longing?

A Testable Strategy

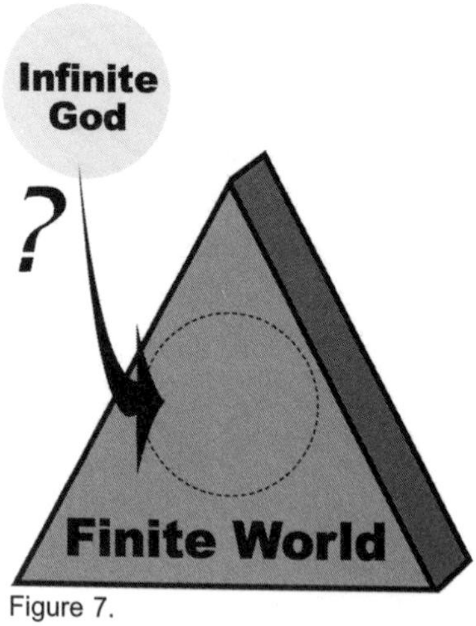

The answer to me was simple. If there were a real God, the one way that I could know this for certain would be for Him to become visible and tangible—able to be seen, heard and touched. I wanted to see Him in real history on planet earth. That would also answer the objection against God by the atheist Flew. Subsequently, I have come to realize that this line of thinking was appropriate. I see it

Figure 7.

now in terms of the triangle illustration: Is it conceivable that the circle (God) might become visible and tangible within the triangle (finite world) of soil, grass, cows and people?

Two Essential Characteristics of God

Analysis during the years since my original struggle has given me additional insight. The writings of the late Dr.

> "If God does not exist... man is in consequence forlorn, for he cannot find anything to depend upon, either within or outside himself."
>
> Jean Paul Sartre, French existentialist philosopher

Francis Schaeffer, philosopher and theologian, have been particularly helpful. He argued that not just any God will do. A God who would be adequate to solve the problem of purpose and meaning, and thereby explain man's personal nature, would have to possess certain characteristics. In particular, two are critical. [7]

1. God must be *infinite*

An infinite and eternal God is one who by definition is complete and entirely perfect, lacking nothing. This God must exist before and outside the finite triangle or I could rightly ask, "What is God's purpose?" Being infinite makes such a question of God meaningless since He is not dependent on anything else. If purpose were not inherent in His being, He would not be infinite. Likewise, if God were not infinite, He would be of no help in solving the problem of purpose and meaning for us inside the triangle, because He too would be part of the problem. Furthermore, He would be incapable of creating the triangle and placing it in space in the first place.

2. God must be *personal*

Personal beings communicate, build relationships and are capable of love. They have rational, intellectual ability, a will and emotions. They are not like the wind, fire or a radar beam. None of these can reciprocate my affection.

Likewise, the impersonal "Force" of *Star Wars* fame will never suffice for God. It is conceivable to imagine a force (god) that raps everyone on earth alongside the head every day at noon. We would all know that something was really there and everyone would probably be conditioned to "duck" every day at noon. We could be conditioned like Pavlov's dog. But we could not understand why we are being struck (Is it a "love pat" or a punishment?) or how to appease this force's actions. Some form of rational, specified and clarifying communication would be necessary, and we know that only personal beings are capable of that. A personal being capable of this kind of communication and love could establish a relationship with us. But this is not so with a concept of God as a "universal, impersonal spirit." Only a God who was "someone" rather than "something" could come into the triangle and be seen, touched and understood.

World Religions on Trial

People throughout the finite triangle, which is our world, claim to know there is a God. But they do not agree at all on what He is like. With a broad brush, all the religions can be classified according to their views on the two essential characteristics of God identified above. They fall into three basic categories.

Eastern Thought

Religions such as Buddhism and Hinduism maintain that God is indeed infinite. God is the source and sustainer of all that exists. But the Eastern God is not a personal being. Instead, they say that all is God and God is all. This is

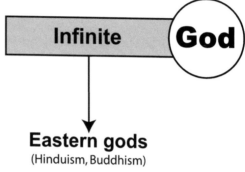

Eastern gods
(Hinduism, Buddhism)

Figure 8.

the basis for New Age teaching that humans are divine since they are part of the "all." However, in Eastern thought about God there is no person there — no rational ability, no emotion, no love, no communication. There is no one to get to know. God is an impersonal, cosmic presence, not someone to see, hear or touch. God is infinite, yet impersonal, like the wind.

Furthermore, an impersonal God does not provide a basis for moral questions of good and evil. In Hinduism, there is both a good and a bad force. But since "all is one," nothing is ultimately right or wrong.

Also, Hinduism doesn't answer the question, "How can I be personal? Where do self-awareness, self-consciousness and personhood all come from?" The Hindu would answer, "To know God as impersonal requires that we deny or transcend our own personhood." Chanting "Om" is the pursuit of an altered state of consciousness, an attempt to escape our personhood purposefully, in order to know God, i.e., to become one with the impersonal universe.

Western Thought

The Greeks and Nordic peoples had a different idea. Anyone who has read the mythologies knows that their gods are very personal and knowable beings. They have clear personalities. The dilemma is that these gods have more problems than people do. They are not infinite. They fight, lust and envy —demonstrating that they are finite and in-

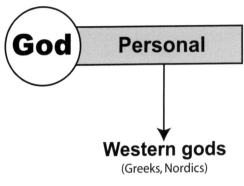

Western gods
(Greeks, Nordics)

Figure 9.

adequate in themselves. They cannot provide ultimate purpose and meaning.

Three Exceptions

What are we to do? The East has religions that claim an infinite God exists, but is not personal (has no intellect, will or emotion). I must believe such a God exists, but from within the finite triangle in which I exist, I have no way to know or establish a relationship with such a God.

The West has religions that claim personal gods that are knowable but inadequate. The Western gods are not infinite and cannot offer an answer to ultimate purpose and meaning, i.e., how we got here, why we are here, and what our final destiny is.

There are, however, three religions that claim their God is both infinite *and* personal. Judaism, Christianity and Islam all teach that God is both the infinite Creator and a personal Being with rational ability, will and emotion, Who is knowable.

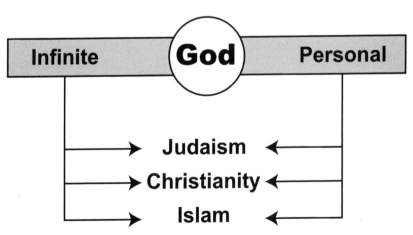

Figure 10.

The Critical Difference

How would each of these religions respond to the question, "How can I know that your God really exists?"

Judaism would say that God revealed Himself to the prophet Moses with verbal communication detailed in the first five books of the Old Testament (the Pentateuch). Such a specified message could only come from a personal Being with intellect. Furthermore, their God claims in these writings to be eternal and the infinite Creator of the universe. Thus, the Jewish God is believed to be both infinite and personal.

Islam would say the same except that their specified message, the Koran, came through Muhammad. Both prophets claim to get their writings from God, but the writings contradict each other. Thus, some would say that the two messages are not from God at all—certainly not from the same One because that would suggest that God is confused! The atheist, Dr. Flew, would still likely object that such an invisible and elusive God could be humanly contrived.

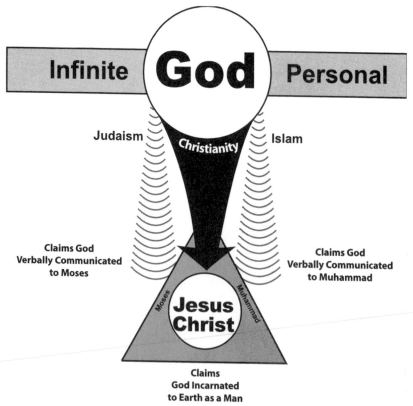

Figure 11.

How would Christians answer the question? Christianity alone goes beyond the belief that God exists and that He communicated with specified messages, to the claim that the infinite and personal God came to earth as a physical man, Jesus Christ. In other words, the circle (God) came into the triangle (world) where he could be seen, heard and handled. For Christians, God did not remain invisible and intangible. Only Christianity claims that its founder is God incarnate, not just a prophet or holy man. Because God became a human being and lived for more than thirty years on the earth, He affords everyone a unique opportunity to test this critical difference, that is, to test the Christian answer to how we know that God really exists.

> "The Christian claim that the whole and only meaning of history before and after Christ rests on the historical appearance of Jesus Christ is a claim so strange, stupendous, and radical that it could not and cannot but contradict and upset the normal historical consciousness of ancient and modern times."
> Karl Lowith, Meaning in History

Jesus either *is* or is *not* God as Christians claim Him to be. You don't have to just blindly believe this allegation. You can investigate this person with the same logic and reason that are applied to other historical studies. This is truly a testable claim.

CONDITIONS FOR A REASONABLE TESTING OF THE CLAIM THAT JESUS IS GOD

I wish that my own path in pursuit of God had been this clear to me at the time. Rather, I meandered through books of science, philosophy and religion, trying to find my way. Eventually I did find, in personal experience, the route outlined here. For the reader who is wondering right now if God can be found, I believe I can save you considerable time and frustration. There is hope and excitement ahead for you. Christianity claims that God *has* made Himself available to be known in the natural world of reason and evidence. The allegation that the infinite-personal Creator of the world had become a man, Jesus of Nazareth, is a claim that can be tested. To do so, there are three conditions that must be met.

A Trustworthy First-Century Historical Record

The first condition is readily apparent. The visit by God occurred some 2,000 years ago. How can anyone today be sure it really happened and that Jesus was a real person of history? To test this Christian claim would require the existence of written records of Jesus. The only known records that are detailed enough for this test are the writings of the New Testament. My view at the time was that the Gospel accounts of Matthew, Mark, Luke and John contained legendary stories reworked over the centuries and distorted by translators, so that little remained of authentic history. Indeed, a feature story in *Time* magazine stated that 82% of what the Gospels attribute to Jesus' life and teachings are legends.[8] In other words, I didn't believe the Bible was true. I felt that way even though I had never investigated the literary evidence concerning the New Testament's integrity or its historical reliability.

The first condition, then, for testing the claim that Jesus was God incarnate is the need for a trustworthy first-century historical record of Jesus. How else could anyone reasonably form a firsthand conviction concerning Jesus if they had no eyewitness sources? The first pursuit, then, is to determine whether the New Testament is reliable as a source of first century history.

A Method of Proof

> "I cannot make my peace with the randomness doctrine: I cannot abide the notion of purposelessness and blind chance in nature. And yet I do not know what to put in its place for the quieting of my mind... We talk—some of us anyway—about the absurdity of the human situation, but we do this because we do not know how we fit in, or what we are for."
> Lewis Thomas, *On the Uncertainty of Science*

Secondly, in any intellectual pursuit there must be some means of fact gathering. Furthermore, there has to be some agreement on what would constitute an adequate proof of the claim that Jesus is God. The scientific method was clearly the method of choice in observing the natural world. But it requires that the experiment be repeatable in a controlled environment so it can be observed. History is not repeatable and does not lend itself to the scientific method. Neither do beauty, aesthetic values, nor a host of other matters. How do you prove something that is a one-time event?

We routinely accept another method of proof for historical events. It is the legal method with our system of courts, judges and juries. A case of evidence is presented by both the prosecution and the defense concerning the issue being tried. A judge or a jury weighs the evidence and makes a reasonable judgment or decision concerning the issue.

This rational approach to gathering the data and weighing its validity is the way to approach the evidence concerning the New Testament and the person of Jesus. Since the New Testament claims to be an eyewitness document of history, the second condition for testing its claims must be using the legal method. You, the reader, will be both the judge and the jury in declaring a verdict based on the evidence.

An Honest Skepticism

If faith in God is to be more than anti-intellectual and emotion-based, it has to be willing to test biblical claims using the legal method. By these means it is able to scrutinize Christianity's claim that Jesus was the incarnation of God. But a third condition must be in place as well: You, the reader, must be honest and objective with the evidence. The humorous story of a dishonest skeptic illustrates why this is necessary.

A man unexpectedly began telling his family, neighbors and co-workers that he was dead. When his wife took him to a local psychiatrist, he was given the task of researching the medical school books and journals until he had a firm conviction on the question, "Do dead people bleed?" After weeks of reading he returned with the verdict that the evidence was overwhelming—dead people do not bleed. The psychiatrist smiled and grabbed a pin he had set aside for this very moment. He mercilessly poked the man's finger, and waited for his response. The man stared at the blood dripping from his finger, turned ashen white and exclaimed, "Dead people do bleed!"

That man was a dishonest skeptic. Many ask for answers to their questions about faith, answers that are based on facts and evidence. It is equally important that their response to those answers and that evidence be an honest one. Using the legal method of testing the claim that God became incarnate as a man on planet earth would be futile if one's attitude was, "Don't confuse me with the facts. My mind is already made up."

— FOCUS & DISCUSSION —

1. Can you relate to any of the caricatures about faith mentioned in this chapter? How have caricatures and bad examples of religious people affected your attitudes and personal impressions of faith?

2. What factors, intellectual or otherwise, may cause some people not to believe in God?

3. When everything is going well for people, what kinds of things will they identify as satisfying their need for purpose and meaning?

4. Muslims and Jews claim to know God through messages He gave to prophets, but Christians claim to know God because He also walked the earth as a human. Why is the difference in these two views significant when it comes to testing for the existence of God?

5. Which can be used in a court of law: an eyewitness account or hearsay? Why? How is this important to the first condition identified as necessary to test legally the claim that Jesus is God?

6. Do you agree that the validity of the Christian faith can be explored rationally? Why or why not?

CHAPTER 2

IS THE BIBLE TRUE?

The Tests of Integrity and Historical Reliability

"The historical Bible (the written Word) and Jesus Christ (the living Word) are the two cornerstones of the Christian worldview. If the Bible is not history or if Jesus Christ is not "God with us" (Matthew 1:23), Christianity crumbles. To shatter Christian doctrine and the Christian worldview, one need only shatter its historical underpinnings..."
David A. Noebel (*Understanding the Times*)

"The test of truth is the known factual evidence..."
Jacob Bronowski (*Science and Human Values*)

One of the most basic Christian truth claims is that Jesus Christ was God in human flesh, the highest, most illuminating revelation of God to man. It is further claimed that Jesus revealed to all who knew Him, by what He said and did, that He was the unique Son of God. This is what we want to test.

The difficulty is not in recognizing the historical reality of a man called Jesus of Nazareth, for that is assured by several recognized extra-biblical sources.[1] Historical research scholar, Dr. Edwin Yamauchi, sets the record straight on this: "From time to time some people have tried to deny the existence of Jesus, but this is really a lost cause...There is overwhelming evidence that Jesus did exist..."[2] The difficulty is that the only detailed biography of this man Jesus are the biblical Gospel sources of Matthew, Mark, Luke and John. Are these records credible, i.e., are they an authentic and historically reliable record of the words and deeds of Jesus?

A serious, yet amusing, commentary on this question was written to syndicated columnist, Ann Landers. It is extreme in its wording, but not unique in the opinion expressed.

> Dear Ann: Please, for heaven's sake, stop pushing religion! Anyone with half a brain knows that your readers are, for the most part, simple-minded, superstitious dimwits who can't face life without a crutch. But doesn't it bother you when you advise about the laws of God — a 2,000-year-old fairy tale? One day I hope you write a column denouncing the God myth and then quit! The ultimate limit of human foolishness, the most pre-posterous bit of irrational hokum ever dreamed up by human kind is the baloney found in the scriptures. Such nonsense is for weaklings and idiots who are unable to think for themselves or accept responsibility for their own actions.[3]

If this commentary were valid, there would be little hope of forming a reasonable and objective personal conviction concerning the claim that Jesus was God. Is this writer's position supported by evidence?

TESTING THE INTEGRITY OF THE NEW TESTAMENT

The testing of ancient documents for integrity is a common practice among literary scholars. There is a large body of literature, written both earlier and later than the New Testament, where integrity is also an issue. For example, the histories of Herodotus and Caesar (5th and 1st centuries B.C., respectively) are well known. Tacitus and Josephus wrote histories of Rome and of the Jews, respectively, about the end of the first century A.D. The criteria for testing such literature for integrity are well known among scholars. Therefore, there is no need to create anything new for examination of the New Testament writings. We need only to apply already accepted criteria.

Because this is unfamiliar ground for most, it is necessary to imagine an ancient scenario to understand the issues. There is a well-known work written about 50 B.C. entitled *The Gallic Wars*.[4] These are the personal memoirs of Julius Caesar's brilliant military campaigns. Let us suppose shortly after they were written that a friend of Caesar was visiting the palace, noted the work, and requested a copy for his own library.

Caesar granted his request, but there was no photocopier in his office and no digital copy to send attached to an e-mail. Instead, the friend needed to send for a trained copyist who would labor for days to hand-write every letter, word and sentence. Would the copy be exactly like Caesar's original? That is unlikely.

Now a person visits the home of Caesar's friend, notes his copy of *The Gallic Wars*, and secures permission to have his copyist come in to make a second generation copy for himself. Will it be exactly like the first generation copy? That is also unlikely. Therefore, it will likely have even more changes from Caesar's original. To the extent that changes occur in the copies, is the extent to which the work has lost some of its integrity. So far the changes are probably minor, but multiply that scenario by hundreds of generations over centuries of time. The integrity is certain to degenerate. By the time we reach the fifteenth century and put the copies of that generation onto Gutenberg's newly-invented printing press, it is possible that only a shadow of Caesar's original writing may remain.

But why not just refer back to Caesar's original writing? Why rely on copies at all if we can go to the autograph (the handwritten original)? The answer is simple: there are no autographs. Not only has Caesar's original never been found, but neither have the autographs of any other ancient document, including the New Testament writings. Therefore, we must work from whatever copies have been found, thereby requiring some guidelines to determine their degree of integrity.

Three Questions

The test of integrity determines whether the New Testament Gospels originated in the eyewitness generation of Jesus, and whether these accounts were transmitted to us over the centuries without major changes. Specifically, we need to know if the twenty-first century English New Testament is a reasonably accurate reproduction of the original first-century Greek New Testament. There are three primary questions scholars ask of ancient literature to determine this.

1. How Many Manuscripts Have Been Found?

The first question concerns the number of handwritten copies that have been found, that is, the manuscript evidence. The more abundant the number of ancient copies that are found, the better. Even if there are variant readings, a large number of copies allows comparison and correlation in order to better restore the original text. Furthermore, a large number of manuscripts over the centuries minimizes the possibility that a little band of people created the documents "behind closed doors," so to speak. A large number of copies means broader public exposure and greater accountability to integrity.

As a youth I knew virtually nothing about manuscript studies. My first exposure, though quite limited, came during college. In my skepticism, I remember thinking that it was probably certain that the New Testament evidence would be quite inferior to that of the writings of the great classical writers such as Plato, Homer or Aristotle. Later in graduate school I discovered, to my surprise, that the New Testament is vastly superior. Additional study over the years has enhanced my understanding of this academic discipline. These later insights are included throughout this chapter to give the reader a greater understanding of the evidence for the first condition needed to test the Christian claim about Jesus.

How many manuscript copies of ancient works are available for study today?[5] Obviously, to know a work existed we would need to have found at least one. The 643 manuscript copies of Homer's *Iliad* that exist is an exceptional example among ancient works. Most have manuscript copies numbering only in the single and double digits. There are only about ten manuscripts ever found of Caesar's *The Gallic Wars*, seven for Plato's *Tetralogies*, twenty for Livy's *History of Rome*, and only a couple for Tacitus' minor works.

What about the New Testament? There are more than 5,664 known manuscripts in the original Greek language. There are, in addition, some 18,000 ancient New Testament manuscripts in Latin, Syriac, Ethiopic, Armenian and other language versions, together with New Testament text found in ancient hymn books (lectionaries) of the early church. All together, about 24,000 handwritten copies of portions of the New Testament have survived.[6] British scholar F.F. Bruce concludes from the data, "There is no body of ancient literature in the world which enjoys such a wealth of good textual attestation as the New Testament."[7] Figure 1 shows the extreme contrast between the manuscript evidence for the New Testament and that of other selected ancient writings.

The comparison is not even close. So much for my reasonable certainty that the New Testament would not fare well under scrutiny! When my reading during graduate school exposed me to these facts, I realized that I had been dishonest. I never questioned, or even examined, the accuracy of the ancient texts of other works that I read. But I somehow *knew* the New Testament text could not be trusted, and

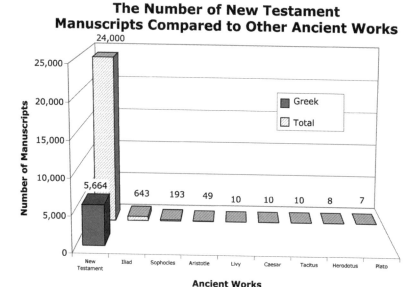

The Number of New Testament Manuscripts Compared to Other Ancient Works

Figure 1.

feigned intellectual reasons for my distrust. However, my ignorance was the real culprit. Later in my career, when reading Sir Frederic Kenyon, eminent scholar of textual criticism, I found out that I had not been alone in holding this double standard:

> Scholars are satisfied that they possess substantially the true text of the principal Greek and Roman writers whose works have come down to us, of Sophocles, of Thucydides, of Cicero, of Virgil; yet our knowledge of their writings depends on a mere handful of manuscripts, whereas the manuscripts of the New Testament are counted by hundreds, and even thousands.[8]

2. How Early Are The Manuscripts?

The second issue affecting integrity is the date when the discovered manuscripts had been copied. Obviously, the further removed in time the copies are from the originals, the more likely they are to have accumulated copyist errors, additions and deletions, i.e., to have less integrity. Fortunately, while the total number of these errors is greater simply because of the large number of New Testament manuscripts, the large number of manuscripts also increases proportionately the means for detecting such errors and restoring the original wording.

How close to the authorship do archaeologists actually find ancient manuscript copies? Caesar's *Gallic Wars* was authored about 50 B.C., yet we have no manuscripts available for study today which were copied before the ninth century — a gap of over 900 years. Most of the Greek writings have even greater gaps (1,000-1,500 years), while the Latin works have somewhat less. The shortest span of any generally accepted ancient work is probably that of Virgil, about 300 years between his authorship and the oldest known copy.[9] However, such a short time period is not at all typical.[10] People are troubled when they discover that there are no preserved copies of classical works for hundreds of years after the date of original composition. But they are astonished when they see the data concerning the New Testament.

It is generally agreed that the 27 books and letters of the New Testament were penned over a fifty-year period, beginning approximately A.D. 47. For ease in calculations, I will use the year A.D. 100 as the latest possible date for their completion. What is the earliest copy ever found? Remember, the range for all other literature is 300 to more than 1,500 years after authorship. The John Rylands papyrus, designated by scholars as P52, is a fragment containing a few verses of the New Testament Gospel of John, dating about A.D. 125. This is only some 35 years after the original Gospel had been written by the apostle. Whoever used this copy could have known the author, or even been personally taught by the apostle John, himself.

Furthermore, a strong case has been made recently by Dr. Young Kyu Kim, a manuscript scholar, that the Chester Beatty Papyrus (P46), containing all of Paul's epistles except the pastorals, should be redated to the late first century. This is only about 20 years after the apostle died![11]

But that's not all. Studies of the late-first and early-second century extant writings of those who were students of the eyewitness apostles (e.g., Polycarp, Clement of Rome, Ignatius) reveal extensive references to New Testament writings. For example, about A.D. 96, Clement of Rome refers to the Gospels of Matthew, Mark and Luke, and eight other New Testament letters. Obviously, they must have been written some time before that date in order for Clement to cite them.[12]

Supporting that conclusion are the recently analyzed fragments of Matthew (Magdalen Papyrus), a scroll fragment of Mark at Qumran, and a papyrus fragment of Luke in a Paris library that have been dated by some scholars between A.D. 50 and A.D. 70.[13] Since Jesus lived at least until A.D. 30, these copies were made by people who were contemporaries of Jesus—people who knew Him personally or talked with those who did. While these three manuscripts are all fragments, they never-

Used by permission. The President and Fellows of Magdalen College, Oxford

MAGDALEN MANUSCRIPT
Allegedly the oldest known manuscript of the New Testament—a fragment of Matthew 26. Dated by papyrologist Dr. Carsten Peter Thiede at about A.D. 60.

theless demonstrate that the Gospels were in written form very early. They did not go through a long period of oral transmission during which they took on legendary traditions. No other ancient writing can trace its manuscript copies all the way back to the generation of the eyewitnesses and its original authors!

However, a find consisting of more-complete Gospels would be needed to do textual studies. The Bodmer and Chester Beatty papyri, dating from about A.D. 150-200, exceed every demand. P45, P66 and P75 contain complete copies of the Gospels, including the miracles of Jesus and the details of His resurrection, within 100 years of the originals.[14] Kenyon's commentary on the significance of these manuscripts contradicts many people's perception of what is true regarding the New Testament records.

> The net result of this discovery...is, in fact, to reduce the gap between the earlier manuscripts and the traditional dates of the New Testament books so far that it becomes negligible in any discussion of their authenticity. No other ancient book has anything like such early and plentiful testimony to its text, and no unbiased scholar would deny that the text that has come down to us is substantially sound.[15]

Figure 2 (below) compares several ancient works with the New Testament in regard to the time interval between the original author-

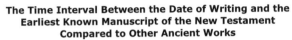

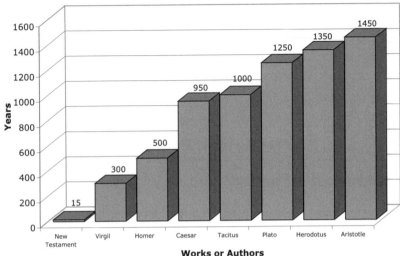

Figure 2.

ship and the earliest extant copies.

Again, the New Testament stands far above all other ancient writings in both the number of manuscripts and the short time span between authorship and the earliest extant copies. There is a nearly continuous chain of copies from the time of the first-century originals to the fifteenth-century printing press. If it were alleged that the text we have today is not essentially like the original autographs, when could they have become corrupted? There are similar copies in every century back to the eyewitnesses. Based on this evidence, the conclusion of scholar F.F. Bruce is certainly justified:

> The evidence for our New Testament writings is ever so much greater than the evidence for many writings of classical authors, the authenticity of which no-one dreams of questioning. And if the New Testament were a collection of secular writings, their authenticity would generally be regarded as beyond all doubt.[16]

3. How Accurately Were The Manuscripts Copied?

The final question measures the extent of distortion of the text due to copying over the centuries. I have already shared the history of my former contention that the text of the New Testament must have been quite significantly muddled by insertions, interpretations and translation. Scholars refer to this as distortion of the meaning of the text. Several people reading such different manuscripts would necessarily arrive at diverse understandings.

Dr. Bruce Metzger, professor of New Testament language and literature at Princeton, published an analysis on this very question. He compared research into the many manuscripts of three ancient works: Homer's *Iliad*, a religious work of the ancient Greeks; the *Mahabharata*, a religious book of Hinduism; and the Christian New Testament.[17] The works varied in length from 15,600 lines for the *Iliad*, 20,000 for the New Testament, and 250,000 for the *Mahabharata*. Variations such as spelling differences, word order, etc., that did not affect the meaning of the text, were ignored. All differences in the manuscripts affecting the reader's understanding were counted. How much distortion did he find?

Dr. Metzger summarized that 764 lines of the *Iliad* were corrupted, a distortion rate of about 5%. Said another way, the meaning of one out of every twenty lines is uncertain. Which *Iliad* do we read in literature class? Who decided which ancient manuscript was the correct one? Yet, it is probably rare that an instructor would caution students about the integrity of the *Iliad* when it is assigned or discussed in class. Its integrity is assumed without question.

The *Mahabharata* was even worse with at least 26,000 lines corrupted, somewhat more than a 10% distortion rate. One out of every ten lines of this religious book was "up for grabs," so to speak. This is not a very reliable source on which to base your life or destiny!

The data for the New Testament, on the other hand, is incredible. Only 40 of 20,000 lines, or 1/5 of 1% (0.2%), are distorted.[18] This is 1/25th of the distortion found in the *Iliad*, which itself has a low distortion rate among ancient writings. Further, F.F. Bruce has said that "the variant readings about which any doubt remains among textual critics of the New Testament affect no material question of historic fact or of Christian faith and practice."[19] Said more simply, no teaching of the Christian faith is in question as a result of the distortion of the New Testament text due to copying over many centuries. Where was the textual confusion that I felt made the New Testament so unacceptable to me during my college years? Figure 3 summarizes Metzger's analysis.

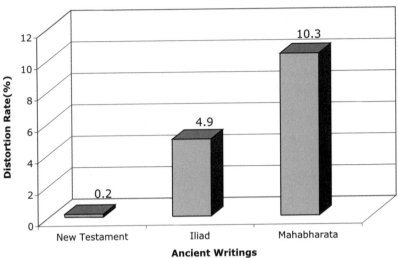

A Comparison of the Rate of Distortion of
Manuscripts Due to Copying Errors

Figure 3.

The Evidence of New Testament Quotes in Other Ancient Writings

There is an additional strong argument for the integrity of the New Testament. The extant writings of the church fathers of the first three centuries after Christ contain over 36,000 quotations or allusions to New Testament books.[20] These quotations make it possible to reconstruct the early New Testament text today even if no New Testament manuscript copies had survived. Indeed, Dr. Metzger says that "so extensive are these citations that if all other sources for our knowledge of the text of the New Testament were destroyed, they would be sufficient alone for the reconstruction of practically the entire New Testament."[21]

Textual scholar Kenyon states this truth another way:

It cannot be too strongly asserted that in substance the text of the Bible is certain: Especially is this the case with the New Testament. The number of manuscripts of the New Testament, of early translations from it, and of quotations from it in the oldest writers of the Church, is so large that it is practically certain that the true reading of every doubtful passage is preserved in some one or other of these ancient authorities. This can be said of no other ancient book in the world.[22]

The weight of this evidence would have been very significant for me when I was wrestling with these issues. Unfortunately, at that time I didn't know about it. But it was exposure to this evidence during graduate school that began a revolution in my thinking. Subsequently, I have become persuaded that when I pick up my current copy of the New Testament records of Jesus' life, it is essentially the same as when the eyewitnesses wrote it 2,000 years ago in the first century A.D. This was the earlier conclusion of researcher and scholar Kenyon:

> ...[T]he last foundation for any doubt that the Scriptures have come down to us substantially as they were written has now been removed. Both the authenticity and the general integrity of the books of the New Testament may be regarded as finally established.[23]

But how can someone know that what the first-century writers wrote is true? Maybe Matthew liked to write fairy tales. Just because we have an authentic record of the first-century New Testament writings doesn't guarantee that it is history. It could be myth. So far I have only demonstrated that the New Testament in comparison with all other ancient writings 1) has more manuscripts, 2) has earlier manuscripts, and 3) is more-accurately copied. But how can a person today know that what the original authors wrote about really happened as they described it?

TESTING THE HISTORICAL RELIABILITY OF THE NEW TESTAMENT

Testing the truthfulness of the New Testament records requires some independent sources that would substantiate its historical accuracy. There is also a need to learn more about the New Testament documents and their authors within the historical context of the first century. Are the documents internally consistent? These are issues addressed routinely in literary criticism.

The External Evidence

It is well known that there are many references in the New Testament records to allegedly historical people (e.g., Pontius Pilate, Gallio and Caesar Augustus), to places (e.g., Jericho, Egypt and the Sea of Galilee), and to events (e.g. the Roman census, the crucifixion of Jesus and a Palestinian drought). Indeed, Luke, traditional author of one of the Gospels and the Acts of the Apostles, consistently casts his writings in a historical context, for example: "In the fifteenth year of the reign of Tiberius Caesar—when Pontius Pilate was governor of Judea, Herod tetrarch of Galilee, his brother Philip tetrarch of Iturea and Traconitis, and Lysanias tetrarch of Abilene — during the high priesthood of Annas and Caiaphas..."[24] This is a real plus for our test purposes, as scholar F. F. Bruce points out: "A writer who thus relates his story to the wider context of world history is courting trouble if he is not careful; he affords his critical readers so many opportunities for testing his accuracy. Luke takes this risk and stands the test admirably."[25] What evidence led Bruce to that conclusion?

The Evidence of Archaeology

One of the most fruitful sources in this regard is the findings in the field of archaeology. Volumes have been written on specific details, mostly in the twentieth century. Scientific archaeology is really only a century and a half old. British scientists first pioneered the modern techniques that have led to a revolution of knowledge about ancient times. Perhaps it is safe to say that because of modern archaeology, more is known today about first century New Testament background than anyone has known about it since the third century. With so much data available today, it is no longer difficult to test the New Testament's claim to historicity.

James, son of Joseph, brother of Jesus

Hailed by *Time* magazine as the "most important discovery in the history of New Testament archaeology,"[26] a limestone bone box or ossuary that may once have contained the bones of James, the brother of Jesus, was discovered in 2002 in Jerusalem.[27] James is identified in the New Testament as one of the brothers of Jesus[28] and later as the leader of the Jerusalem church.[29] But the reason this discovery made the front page of *The New York Times* and nearly every other newspaper in the world is that it bore an inscription in clear Aramaic letters: "James, son of Joseph, brother of Jesus." Archaeologists believe it is "the earliest archaeological attestation of three important figures—Jesus, James and Joseph—in the history of Christianity."[30] James was martyred in A.D. 62. Tests on the limestone of the box, expert examination of the inscription, and the writing style all support its origin during the time period in which James died. Because it is a very recent discovery, there

JAMES BONE BOX BAS
Recently discovered first century burial box (ossuary) with the inscription: "James, son of Joseph, brother of Jesus."

are skeptics and scholars who feel additional study on the ossuary will be necessary to confirm its authenticity.[31] If it should hold up to this scrutiny, it would be an enormously important affirmation of the New Testament's historical truthfulness in its references to both Jesus and his family.

Pontius Pilate and Caiaphas

Pilate, identified in the New Testament Gospel accounts as the governor of Judea at the time of Christ's crucifixion, is confirmed by references to him in writings of the Jewish historian Josephus and the Roman historian Tacitus.[32] Additional confirmation came when archaeological excavation of the site of ancient Caesarea Maritima, the city from which he ruled, uncovered a two-by-three-foot cornerstone near the theater with the inscription: "Pontius Pilate, the Prefect of Judea, has dedicated to the people of Caesarea a temple in honor of Tiberius."[33]

Likewise, the Gospel of Luke mentions Caiaphas as the Jewish high priest who presided over the trial of Jesus.[34] In 1990, during road construction in Jerusalem, heavy equipment broke through the roof of a limestone cave or tomb used for burial in the first century. Located in the Peace Forest, the cave contained a sculptured bone box, or ossuary,

Dr. Boyd Seevers

CAESAREA STONE OF PONTIUS PILATE

A building stone found in the city of Caesarea with an inscription that documents the historicity of both Pontius Pilate and Tiberius.

with a name inscribed on the side. It was "Joseph Caiaphas," the same high priest mentioned by Luke.[35] A tomb nearby likely belonging to the high priest Annas has also been found.[36]

These people and many others such as kings Herod the Great and Herod Agrippa II, emperors Augustus and Tiberius, and rulers Gallio and Sergius Paulus are part of the continuing discoveries of archaeology proving that the New Testament references are to real historical persons, not the product of legends.

The Roman Census and Date of Jesus' Birth

"In those days Caesar Augustus issued a decree that a census should be taken of the entire Roman world. (This was the first census that took place while Quirinius was governor of Syria.)"[37] For many years the existence of a Roman census was questioned by critics of the New Testament. But papyrus census forms have been found dating from the first centuries B.C. and A.D., proving the practice was common during Jesus' lifetime and in His locality.[38]

But when it was discovered that the Roman Empire conducted its census only every fourteen years, critics said it didn't correspond to the year of Jesus' birth. Furthermore, the only time that anyone knew of a Quirinius being governor of Syria was A.D. 6. However, recent external evidence has again confirmed the historical accuracy of the New Testament.

We now know that King Herod the Great died in the spring of 4 B.C. and he was very much alive when Jesus was born. Based on this fact and that Jesus was "about thirty" when he began His ministry in A.D. 26, Jesus' birth must have been in the winter of 5-4 B.C.[39] How did we get it wrong? A sixth-century Roman monk dated the Nativity in the 753rd year from the founding of Rome, but his chronology was off by four to five years. Unfortunately his errant chronology was adopted in the Gregorian calendar, which is still used today.

But what about the problem of Quirinius and the timing of the census? Archaeologist Sir William Ramsay found several inscriptions indicating that a Quirinius was indeed governor of Syria on two occasions. The first was several years previous to his appointment to that position by Augustus in A.D. 6. A Quirinius has recently been found on an ancient coin that has him as proconsul of Syria and Cilicia from 11 B.C. until after 4 B.C.[40] He would have been the governor at Jesus' birth in 5 B.C. and the date of the biblical Roman census is now thought by many to have been conducted from 8 B.C. through 5 B.C., with the later time likely for an outlying area like Palestine. Again, this corresponds in time with the year of Jesus' birth. Even though the traditional year of Jesus' birth is certainly incorrect, His birth has nevertheless served as the anchor for the designations B.C. and A.D. for nearly everyone in the whole world for centuries.[41]

Jesus' Ministry

The existence of numerous specific cites that are referenced in the Gospels have been confirmed by archaeologists. The remains of a first-century house located under a fourth-century church in Capernaum is believed to be that of the apostle Peter, and where Jesus often stayed during his Galilean ministry. Sometime in the middle of the first cen-

Jerry Hawkes at www.holylandphotos.org

CAPERNAUM SYNAGOGUE
The remains of this third or fourth century synagogue in Capernaum, built over the one in which Jesus taught. The first century floor was 60' x 79' and is visible as the black basalt layer (see inset).

www.holylandphotos.org

tury it apparently was converted from a residence to a chapel that was set apart for public viewing and use. Likewise in Capernaum, the 60 x 79-foot floor of a synagogue dating to the first-century has been discovered.[42] This is the same synagogue the New Testament says was built by a Roman centurion who loved the Jews, and where Jesus often preached during his ministry.[43]

In Jerusalem, excavations along the southern wall of the Temple Mount have uncovered a number of baptisteries used for ritual purification by immersion.[44] These are likely the ones that Luke's Gospel refers to that was used by Joseph and Mary before going onto the Temple Mount for Mary's purification after giving birth to Jesus.[45] Other external evidence uncovered by archaeologists relating to the historicity of Jesus' ministry is the discovery of the pool of Bethesda in Jerusalem where Jesus healed the invalid,[46] the pool of Siloam at the end of the 1,749-foot-long tunnel of Hezekiah where Jesus restored the sight of a man who was born blind,[47] and the site of Gergesa (modern El Kursi) on the east side of the Sea of Galilee, where Jesus cast the demons out of a man and into a herd of swine.[48] It is an amazing truth that we are able to go today, 2,000 years after Jesus lived, and still see the same places where He walked and ministered!

POOL OF SILOAM www.holylandphotos.org
South of the present walled city is the Pool of Siloam where Jesus sent a blind man to wash and receive his sight.

Crucifixion of Jesus

The Gospel writers refer to the use of nails in the crucifixion of Jesus on a cross of wood. The accuracy of the reported use of nails, as opposed to tying the victim on the cross, and even the practice of crucifixion itself in Palestine, have both been questioned by critics. Surely, they said, the writers must have embellished their stories with unhistorical details. A recent publication suggests not.[49] I read with fascination a scientific article reporting on the only crucifixion victim ever discovered. The remains of a twenty-four- to twenty-eight-year-old man were found in a tomb near Jerusalem with a four-and-one-half to five inch-long nail through his foot.[50] His crucifixion was dated by the carbon-14 method at A.D. 42 (Jesus was crucified about A.D. 30). Once again, archaeology has confirmed the biblical account. They <u>did</u> have nails in Jerusalem at the time of Jesus, and they <u>did</u> use them for crucifixion—just like the Gospel writers reported!

Furthermore, the calf bones of this victim were "brutally fractured... clearly produced by a single, strong blow."[51] This was amazing evidence supporting a Palestinian

CRUCIFIXION VICTIM
Excavation in Jerusalem resulted in the discovery of the ankle and foot bones (and nail) of the only crucifixion victim ever found by archaeologists. The date was close to the time of Jesus' crucifixion. (The sketch above was based on a photograph.)

variation of the Roman practice of crucifixion, as referred to in the Gospel of John: "The soldiers therefore came and broke the legs of the first man who had been crucified with Jesus, and then those of the other. But when they came to Jesus and found that He was already dead, they did not break His legs."[52] The archaeologist explained:

> Normally, the Romans left the crucified person undisturbed to die slowly of sheer physical exhaustion leading to asphyxia. However, Jewish tradition required burial on the day of execution. Therefore, in Palestine the executioner would break the legs of the crucified person in order to hasten his death and thus permit burial before nightfall. This practice, described in the Gospels in reference to the two thieves ... has now been archaeologically confirmed.[53]

Politarchs

During the apostle Paul's second missionary journey he visited the city of Thessalonica. Luke refers to the city officials there by the term "politarchs."[54] The problem was that this title had not been found in other ancient literature, and it was assumed by critics that Luke made up the term because he did not have firsthand knowledge of the area. They were quick to allege that this was an example of the New Testament's inaccurate history. But beginning with William Ramsay, classical scholar and archaeologist at Oxford in the late nineteenth century, at least thirty-two inscriptions have been found by archaeologists that contain this title, nineteen of which come from Thessalonica, three of those from the first century.[55] The most notable was Ramsay's discovery of Greek names under the phrase, "…in the time of the Politarchs" on a stone archway that stood at the entrance into the first-century city of Thessalonica, the same archway that the apostle Paul and Luke would have gone through.

Luke had it right—"politarchs" was the correct title of magistrates in some Macedonian towns. Though frequently questioned, Luke's historical accuracy has been vindicated by archaeological evidence. Indeed, F.F. Bruce says that Luke's "sure familiarity with the proper titles of all the notable persons who are mentioned in his pages" is "one of the most remarkable tokens of his accuracy."[56] He cites several pages of examples. After a lifetime of research, archaeologist William Ramsay acknowledged that the evidence changed his mind from one of skepticism and unbelief to the view "that Luke's history is unsurpassed in respect of its trustworthiness." He identified Luke as "a historian of the first rank," placing him "along with the very greatest of historians."[57]

Archaeological discoveries today are no longer relevant just for a few scientists or the curious adventurer. With the expansion of excavation in Israel and the advent of worldwide communication means like the Internet, people in homes and offices everywhere are becoming aware of the scientific facts that confirm the historical truthfulness of Jesus' life and the beginning of Christianity.

The Testimony of Scholars

The professional judgments of international experts also support the historical accuracy of the New Testament. William Albright, famous archaeologist of Johns Hopkins University, wrote:

> The excessive skepticism shown toward the Bible by important schools of the eighteenth and nineteenth centuries, certain phases of which still appear periodically, has been progressively discredited. Discovery after discovery has established the accuracy of innumerable details, and has brought increased recognition to the value of the Bible as a source of history.[58]

This theme is repeated again and again. For example, Millar Burrows of Yale stated that "archaeological work has unquestionably strengthened confidence in the reliability of the scriptural record. More than one archaeologist has found his respect for the Bible increased by the experience of excavation in Palestine."[59] This is a real challenge for those who demand evidence. To determine the truthfulness of New Testament statements, Dr. Burrows invites them to grab a spade and join him in checking it out! Nelson Glueck, renowned Jewish archaeologist, claimed that "no archaeological discovery has ever controverted a biblical reference."[60]

Finally, Kenyon, considered a foremost authority in this field, expressed what some have thought was an overly optimistic statement: "Archaeology has not yet said its last word, but the results already achieved confirm what faith would suggest, that the Bible can do nothing but gain from an increase in knowledge."[61] While this was written in 1948, Kitchen recently affirmed that the "continuing discoveries and work of the intervening decades have not changed, merely enhanced, the truth of his judgment."[62] So much for my uninformed view that Christianity and faith were anti-intellectual.

> "A young man who wishes to remain a sound Atheist cannot be too careful of his reading. There are traps everywhere— 'Bibles laid open, millions of surprises,' as Herbert says, 'fine nets and stratagems.' God is, if I might say it, very unscrupulous."
>
> C.S. Lewis, Surprised by Joy

The Internal Evidence

Somewhere in my early years I picked up the view that the stories written about Jesus were really legends that had developed long after He was gone. During my college skepticism, I thought that it was naive to believe 2,000-year-old accounts if they were not written by those who lived at the same time as Jesus, and by those who knew Him personally. I couldn't imagine a better source than someone who was actually there.

Eyewitness Authors

Partly at that time, and extensively later, I discovered that this is exactly what the New Testament writers claim for themselves, i.e., that they were eyewitnesses or had eyewitness sources. Furthermore, the Gospel accounts of the words and deeds of Jesus were being proclaimed verbally within fifty days, and had limited circulation in written form within twenty-five years after His death and resurrection. The apostle Peter was able to stand in Jerusalem less than two months after Jesus' death, with those hostile to the Christian movement present, and say, "Men of Israel, listen to these words: 'Jesus the Nazarene, a man attested to you by God with miracles and wonders and signs which God performed through Him in your midst, just as you yourselves know...." He went on to say that "this Jesus God raised up again, to which we are all witnesses,"[63] and there is no indication of any attempts to rebut these appeals to historic fact. Indeed, no one has yet been able to document such a rebuttal.

Imagine the difficulties today of trying to publish a totally fabricated biography of former U.S. president John F. Kennedy. In this fictitious account JFK is depicted as walking on water, healing the sick in front of crowds, raising the dead, and feeding 5,000 people with five barley loaves and two fish. Following his death he was said to be resurrected and then to have ascended to heaven before over 500 eyewitnesses. As a result, a massive religious movement has begun in which JFK is worshipped.

The only way this "biography" could be accepted by the public is if the book never fell into the hands of anyone who knew Mr. Kennedy, or if all who ever knew him were dead, and written accounts of his life and death had been destroyed. Otherwise, those who knew him would testify that it was untrue, as would the written evidence. If there were still a few hardy "believers" in JFK, his body could be exhumed which would put an end to all such nonsense.

> "Faith is not blind... In the case of Christian faith it arose for the earliest disciples from historical contemporaneity with Jesus. They were not compelled by the evidence: plenty of people saw it and declined to commit themselves. But the evidence was the ground on which they committed themselves."
> Michael Green, The Truth of God Incarnate

Likewise, if there were any fabrication or departure from the facts about Jesus on Peter's part, it would be inconceivable that 3,000 would respond in repentance and faith to a person they knew to be a fraud or product of Peter's imagination.[64] This is especially true when we realize that to make such a confession would mean tremendous sacrifice, perhaps the loss of their businesses, their family and even their lives. If Peter knew his statements about Jesus were false, surely he was smart enough to leave Jerusalem and go where people had no firsthand knowledge of Jesus. But Christian teaching about Jesus' life, death and resurrection originated and was accepted in Jerusalem, where the people were in the best position to know whether or not it was true, and where accepting it could cost them dearly.

The apostle Paul, too, with his life on the line before the Roman procurator Festus and King Agrippa, appealed to the events of Jesus' life as historically true. He said, "The king knows about these matters, and I speak to him also with confidence, since I am persuaded that none of these things escaped his notice; for this has not been done in a corner."[65]

Early Date of Writing

Therefore, the extensive evidence that establishes the authorship of the New Testament documents within 20-30 years after Jesus' death makes the theory of legends untenable. As Bruce says, "The disciples could not afford to risk inaccuracies (not to speak of willful manipulation of the facts), which would at once be exposed by those who would be only too glad to do so."[66] No legend is known to have developed and become generally accepted within the same generation as the events and persons themselves.[67] Sherwin-White, Oxford historian of Roman times, explains why: "...[F]or these stories to be legends, the rate of legendary accumulation would have to be 'unbelievable'; more generations are needed... [E]ven the span of two generations is too short to allow legendary tendencies to wipe out the hard core of historical fact."[68]

Legal Proceedings

The legal proceedings against Jesus and Paul mentioned in the trial narratives of the New Testament correspond with what we know of Roman practice during that period of the first century A.D.[69] F.F. Bruce extends the accuracy even "to the more general sphere of local colour and atmosphere. He [Luke] gets the atmosphere right every time."[70] Such subtle inclusions in the New Testament writings could only be the result of authors who were actually there, i.e., eyewitnesses.

A HIGHLY PROBABLE VERDICT

Based on the very methods that literary and historical scholars use today, the only reasonable and logical conclusion that I can draw is that the Bible is the most reliable book of antiquity. If anyone chooses to reject the New Testament evidence as insufficient, honesty to the facts requires that they reject all other ancient literature as well, whose evidence is quite inferior to that supporting the New Testament. For me, only

> "Prejudices are rarely overcome by argument; not being founded in reason they cannot be destroyed by logic."
> Tryon Edwards, *The New Dictionary of Thoughts*

my remaining prejudices caused me to stubbornly cling to my former skeptical views. Had I only known then the more complete evidence that I gained later and have included in this chapter, I do not believe my search would have been as prolonged.

In the eighteenth century the French skeptic Voltaire stated that in one hundred years from his time Christianity would be swept from existence and passed into history. Instead, twenty-five years after his death, the British and Foreign Bible Society was formed and issued over 229,000,000 Bibles in its first 100 years of publishing. Voltaire's own printing press was later used to print copies of the Bible, and the Geneva Bible Society used his home to stack Bibles for distribution.[71] The reliable history on which the Christian faith is based makes it difficult to remove from an informed society. A.N. Sherwin-White, internationally recognized scholar from Oxford, has written that "for [the book of] Acts the confirmation of historicity is overwhelming... any attempt to reject its basic historicity even in matters of detail must now appear absurd. Roman historians have long taken it for granted."[72] He argues similarly for the Gospels. Indeed, Luke makes reference to thirty-two countries, fifty-four cities, and nine islands—without a single mistake.[73]

C.S. Lewis, professor of Medieval and Renaissance Literature at Cambridge University, acknowledged that the evidence for the historicity of the Gospels was a major factor in his conversion from atheism.[74] Frank Morison, an English journalist, set out to prove that the story of Christ was encumbered with legend and myth. He found by his research that the biblical records were historically valid.[75] Scores of others have searched the historical evidence and found it exceedingly convincing.

We have examined some of the evidence supporting the first and crucial condition for testing the claim that Jesus is God; that is, the need for a trustworthy first-century historical record concerning Jesus. The reader is now in the position to be the judge on this matter. We must now turn our focus on what these historically reliable documents report about what Jesus of Nazareth said and did. To determine if He was more than a man will require that we examine these primary sources for the data concerning His life. The jury, as far as that matter is concerned, is still out.

— Focus & Discussion —

1. Why is it so important for the argument of God's existence that the New Testament is a trustworthy first-century historical record?

2. What evidence in this chapter, if any, was unexpected or came as a surprise to you? How did it change your opinion or understanding of the New Testament?

3. Based on the information in this chapter, how has the science of archaeology supported the historical reliability of the New Testament?

4. How well-known in society today is the evidence for the integrity and historical reliability of the New Testament as presented in this chapter? ...in the Christian community? Why do you think this is so?

5. What evidence weakens the allegation that the New Testament accounts of Jesus are only legends?

6. Suppose you were a participant in an event that occurred 25-30 years ago. Can you remember the incident sufficiently to detect a major fabrication of the event if it were presented to you verbally or in print? What implications does this have to the allegation that the Gospel accounts are fabricated legends, not historically true?

IS JESUS REALLY GOD?

Looking At the Eyewitness Evidence

The Archbishop of Canterbury: "Jesus is the Son of God, you know."
Jane Fonda: "Maybe He is for you, but He's not for me."
Archbishop: "Well, either He is or He isn't."
Conversation on the Dick Cavett Show
(in *The Quest for Faith*, C. Stephen Evans)

When a person stops believing in God, he does not believe in nothing.
He will believe in anything.
G.K. Chesterton, British writer

J esus faced a most difficult task. He was born into a Jewish family 2,000 years ago. He grew up in the small town of Nazareth in Israel, a remote and unimportant province of the Roman Empire. By every known indication He grew up as a normal boy who "kept increasing in wisdom and stature, and in favor with God and men."[1] However, when He was about 30 years of age He stood up in the synagogue of His home town and announced, in effect, "There is something I've been meaning to tell you — I'm God!"

If one of my friends or colleagues were to make such a statement, I would either laugh or cry. I would assume he was joking or had lost his mind! What makes Jesus' statement any different? The only way I could seriously consider such a claim is if he were to provide some powerful evidence to back it up. I would need some reasons that prove the guy's credibility.

That is where we are in our test as well. We found in Chapter 2 that we have every reason to trust the Gospel accounts of Jesus' life as reliable sources of history. Therefore, we can use them to test the Christian claim that Jesus is God.

What I am proposing is familiar territory to me. In my professional expertise in the field of ecology, I would occasionally take my students into the field to give them firsthand experience with the lecture subject. That's what I am going to suggest we do with the claim that Jesus is God — take a field trip. We can test the credibility of this claim for ourselves by stepping into the eyewitness' shoes via their accounts, and with their ears hear what He claimed and with their eyes see what He did.

TESTING THE CLAIM THAT GOD BECAME A MAN

Evidence of Jesus' Claims

Messiah[2]

The words that I used above for Jesus' announcement in His hometown were not a quote from the New Testament. Indeed, it could be argued that on that occasion He did not claim deity at all. The incident as recorded in the physician Luke's account indicates that Jesus read from the Old Testament book of the prophet Isaiah.[3] This was a very familiar prophecy that the Jews maintained would be fulfilled by the Messiah, or Christ, when He came. Jesus concluded His reading with the words, "Today this Scripture has been fulfilled in your hearing." In other words, Jesus said, "Here I am, ready or not!" Jesus was claiming to be the prophesied Messiah.[4]

This is a strong claim, and one that He made on other occasions as well.[5] The response of the people who heard Him that day makes this clear: "Is not this Joseph's son?" Their questioning prompted Jesus to anticipate what would be a reasonable expectation under the circumstances when He said, "No doubt you will quote this proverb to Me, 'Physician, heal yourself...'" This was equivalent to our modern expression, "Prove it." It is clear from the context that the people rejected, temporarily at least, Jesus' claim to be the Messiah. Who is right? Only additional evidence can answer this question.

Lord God

Whether or not Jesus was the Messiah paled, however, compared to the issue raised in an encounter that Jesus had with the Pharisees. In it He challenged their teaching that the Messiah was to have only a human nature. Matthew records His reasoning:

> Now while the Pharisees were gathered together, Jesus asked them a question, saying, "What do you think about the Christ, whose son is He?" They said to Him, "The son of David." He said to them, "Then how does David in the Spirit call Him 'Lord,' saying, 'The Lord said to My Lord'... If David then calls Him 'Lord,' how is He his son?" And no one was able to answer Him a word...[6]

The point of the question is that if David in the Old Testament Psalm refers to the Messiah as Lord, then the Messiah must be more than David's physical descendant. The phrase David used is "*Yahweh* [The Lord] said to *Adonai* [My Lord]." Both may be names of God and in English could be translated, "God said to God." David applies the second one to his descendant, the Messiah. Jesus was showing them how inappropriate it would be for David to refer to any other human by the divine title of "Lord." As scholar Tasker states, "In other words, the Messiah, though of Davidic descent, is also of divine origin."[7] Why would Jesus bring this up except to correct an oversight in their teaching concerning the Messiah's nature? Clearly He wanted them to understand that as their Messiah He was both man and God.

I AM[8]

But why was Jesus so subtle? Had He ever come right out and said He was God? That did happen on an occasion when the Jewish leadership asked Him point blank, "Whom do You make Yourself out to be?" Among other things Jesus said, "Truly, truly, I say to you, before Abraham was born, I AM." When we realize that Abraham lived about 2,000 years before Jesus, we can understand their question, "You are not yet fifty years old, and have You seen Abraham?" Jesus is claiming preexistence, that is, He lived before Abraham. Being born a baby in Bethlehem was not His beginning. Indeed, the way He phrased His answer in the present tense suggests that He had no beginning at all.

More importantly, Jesus applied the title "I AM" to Himself. This was one of the names of God from the Old Testament.[9] For a man to do this was unprecedented. The Jewish contemporaries of Jesus were reluctant to even *say* the name of God for fear that their unclean lips might defile it. But Jesus not only put it on His lips, figuratively, He put it on His name tag as well.

The context of the passage further supports this view. Upon hearing His answer, they attempted to stone Jesus to death. This is clear evidence that they understood Him to be claiming deity, since only such a claim would be considered blasphemous and warrant death according to their law.

One with the Father[10]

Jesus was asked to clear up His identity on other occasions as well. At the winter Feast of Dedication in Jerusalem, He was asked again, "How long will You keep us in suspense? If you are the Christ, tell us plainly." Jesus responded, "I and the Father are one." What could He mean by that?

One possibility is that the Father and Jesus are 'one and the same.' This would mean that while Jesus was on earth, there was no one in heaven tending the universe. They are the same person. The grammar of the Greek is helpful here. "One" would need to be in the masculine gender if this was the intended meaning. It is not. It's in the neuter gender.

The neuter gender could mean to be "in agreement" or "in unity." This would be somewhat equivalent to my saying I was in the will of God. But the context of the passage is against that. If that's what Jesus meant, they could not have justified the death penalty, which they clearly sought by attempting to stone Him. Being in unity or agreement with God is what they all should have wanted.

The contemporaries of Jesus, who spoke the same language and shared the same culture, were in the best position to know what He meant by "one." Their understanding is clear in their statement, "For a good work we do not stone You, but for blasphemy; and because You, being a man, make Yourself out to be God." "One" here means "essence," that is, Jesus and the Father are equals. Jesus shares all the divine attributes of the Father. This fits the grammar and the context perfectly, and explains the Pharisees' reaction.

From Above and Not of this World[11]

During the years of my search for answers, I recall thinking that Jesus was, for the most part, quite like any other man. For example, His conversation was wise but didn't seem to me indicative of a claim to deity. I questioned why anyone bothered to attribute deity to Him at all. In hindsight, I realize that I took that position out of ignorance, that is, I really was not acquainted enough with Jesus' teaching to know any better. Later, when I began to read the Gospel records, I realized that many of His statements could never appropriately be a part of any other person's conversation.

Try, for example, to use some of Jesus' words as your own with a neighbor across the backyard fence: "You are from below, I am from above..." Unless you live in an upstairs apartment, you would certainly have his attention. To add Jesus' further words, "You are of this world; I am not of this world," may send your neighbor running — to call 911! These are not the statements of an ordinary man. To claim to be from another world and to add, besides, that unless people believe you are God ("I AM") they will die in their sin and be separated from God forever is to invite scoffing and scorn — unless you can somehow credibly back up your claims.

Give Eternal Life to Anyone[12]

Imagine yourself sitting at a rest island in a busy shopping mall. You beckon several people to you and discretely ask if they would like to live forever. Caught off guard, they stare silently back at you. You assure them that if, after further reflection, eternal life should sound like a good idea, they may look you up and you will grant it to them. I doubt that you would be overwhelmed by the traffic jam at your front door.

But that's exactly what Jesus said—that He could give eternal life to whomever He wished. To Martha and Mary, devastated by the death of their brother, Lazarus, Jesus said, "I am the resurrection and the life; he who believes in Me shall live even if he dies, and everyone who lives and believes in Me shall never die." What makes the difference between His saying it and your or my saying it? Nothing, unless one of us can provide evidence that we can really do it. Jesus did just that — He raised Lazarus from the dead in front of many eyewitnesses.

All Authority in Heaven and on Earth[13]

Imagine going to a conference of world leaders including the president of the United States, and looking them all in the eye and saying, "All authority has been given to Me in heaven and on earth." This is another of Jesus' 'ordinary' human statements that understandably would have been an affront to the great Roman Empire of His day. I believe it is well within the mark to suggest that if some of what Jesus said were put

A SUMMARY OF SELECTED CLAIMS OF JESUS		
1.	**He is the Messiah (Christ)** The Messiah is also identified as "Mighty God" and "Everlasting Father" in Isaiah 9:6.	Luke 4:14-21; John 4:25-26
2.	**He is the Lord God** The Messiah is of Davidic descent and of divine origin.	Matthew 22:41-46
3.	**He is the I AM** He existed before Abraham and can rightly bear the name of God.	John 8:53-59
4.	**He is One with the Father** He is one in "essence" – He possesses all the divine attributes.	John 10:30-33
5.	**He is from above and not of this world** He is of heavenly origin.	John 8:23-24
6.	**He can give eternal life to anyone** He has the right to grant eternal life to His followers and the power to guarantee it.	John 5:21; 10:27-28
7.	**He has all authority in heaven and earth** He is the Son of God with absolute authority in every domain.	Matthew 28:18; John 19:7

Figure 1.

into our mouths today, we would be prime candidates to be locked up or treated for psychological disorders. Indeed, Jesus did die for His claims. Throughout history people have been sentenced for what they do, i.e., for a crime committed. But Jesus was crucified for who He claimed to be: "...He ought to die because He made Himself out to be the Son of God."[14]

There can be little doubt from our field trip thus far, that one of the reasons Christians today think that Jesus is God is because those who were with Him 2,000 years ago report that He claimed to be God. The data of His life recorded by the eyewitnesses is quite convincing. Albert Schweitzer, who himself believed that Jesus misunderstood His own nature, nevertheless acknowledged that the evidence for His claim to be God was good. The concern of his M.D. dissertation at Strasbourg in France was how Jesus could be sane and still claim to be God.[15] Figure 1 summarizes the evidence of Jesus' claims.

Evidence of Jesus' Actions

Many have claimed to be God. Hindu holy men can even draw crowds with alleged magical powers. Invariably, however, their lives fall short of deity and they lose credibility with their followers. Jesus is the exception. The more time people spent with Him, the more certain they were that His claims were valid. This is where the idea of our field trip is particularly valuable. We can see Jesus through the eyes of those who walked with Him. Luke recorded the history of what Jesus did for approximately two years following the people's rejection of His claim in Nazareth. During those two years many changed their minds about Him. Their transformation from skepticism to acceptance is striking. What changed their minds?

The answer to that question is obvious to anyone who takes seriously the history in the biblical accounts of Jesus' life. The eyewitnesses report things He did that were astounding. Many of His contemporaries were persuaded by these events to believe in His divine nature, though they were predisposed against such a conclusion. If we are willing, we can now look for ourselves at what they saw Him do. We will continue our field trip.

Authority to Forgive and Remove the Consequences of Sin[16]

Several of the events that Luke recorded in his Gospel are intriguing. Following His announcement in Nazareth to be the Messiah, Jesus went to Capernaum on the northwest shoreline of the Sea of Galilee. There, in what was likely the apostle Peter's home, many of Israel's most capable religious leaders — Pharisees and lawyers — had gathered. Because the crowd limited access to the site, some men carrying a paralyzed man on a stretcher presented him to Jesus through a hole they tore in the roof of the house. Jesus immediately responded to the paralyzed man, "Friend, your sins are forgiven you." The scribes and Pharisees found that offensive: "Who is this man who speaks blasphemies? Who can forgive sins, but God alone?" What caused them to take offense?

Imagine that while I was speaking to a group, an individual jumped up, rushed to the podium, and knocked me down with a hard blow. Promptly he had a change of heart, apologized profusely, and begged my forgiveness. If I granted it, would the rest of my audience likely accuse me of blasphemy — usurping the prerogative of God? Not only is that unlikely, rather they would likely commend me for my benevolence. Somehow, the circumstances in Jesus' situation must have been different than those in my imaginary scene. Let me try again.

Dr. Boyd Seevers

PETER'S HOME
Just across the street from the Capernaum synagogue, this hexagonal foundation of a fifth century building was built over the still evident remains of the first century home of the apostle Peter.

Once again someone in my audience nearly knocks me out, and apologizes for it. But before I can respond, someone else from my audience comes forward and says to the one who hit me, "I want you to know that I forgive you for hitting Don." Even in my dazed condition, I would certainly question what this third party has to do with it. The offense was against me and it is only right that I should be the one offering forgiveness. This third party neither is in a position to forgive nor had the right to do so. Now to the Pharisees and lawyers, Jesus was this third party. It is unlikely that He ever saw this man before. As far as we know, the man had done nothing to Jesus that required His forgiveness. Whatever sin the paralyzed man had in his life was ultimately an offense against God. Therefore, God should be doing the forgiving! Since the religious leaders had not understood or accepted that Jesus was God, they reasoned that He was guilty of blasphemy in that He, a third party, was usurping the position and right reserved only for God.

Furthermore, they were undoubtedly thinking that this was just idle talk. They didn't believe that He had actually removed the man's sin. After all, it's rather difficult to demonstrate visibly that you have forgiven someone's sins. But in this case there was a way. Luke records Jesus' response to the challenge:

"But, so that you may know that the Son of Man has authority on earth to forgive sins," — He said to the paralytic — "I say to you, get up, and pick up your stretcher and go home." Immediately he got up before them, and picked up what he had been lying on, and went home glorifying God. They were all struck with astonishment... saying, "We have seen remarkable things today."[17]

To instantly heal a paralyzed man and send him home carrying his bed is in itself stunning. But how did this prove that Jesus had taken away the man's sins? The erudite group present there seemed quite persuaded. The answer is found in understanding a certain conviction of the Jews of that day; that is, they saw a direct relationship between sin and consequent judgment in the form of pain, suffering, etc. In the form of an equation, they would say:

Presence of Sin ⇨ Leads to ⇨ Consequence of Sin

In other words, if I were climbing a stairs with a group of first-century Jewish peers, and hurt myself in a fall, they would gather around and ask me what sin I had committed recently! This mindset is illustrated even by Jesus' disciples on another occasion when they asked Jesus whether the plight of a man born blind was caused by his parents' sin or his own.[18] Therefore, when the paralyzed man on the stretcher was brought to Jesus, the religious authorities saw his paralysis as a consequence of his sin. This afforded Jesus an opportunity to visibly demonstrate, to their satisfaction, the removal of the man's sin, i.e., by healing him. If the presence of sin caused the presence of paralysis, the removal of paralysis meant the removal of the sin that caused it.

Removal of the Consequence of Sin ⇨ Proves ⇨ Removal of the Sin that caused it

The Pharisees and lawyers responded, "We have seen remarkable things today." While Jesus used such logic to satisfy their need for overt evidence of His divine power that day, He did not actually share their simplistic view of the relationship between sin and its consequences.[19]

Authority over Death

At the southern Galilean city of Nain, Jesus met a procession en route to taking a widow's only son to burial. Jesus' action is recorded by Luke.

When the Lord saw her, He felt compassion for her, and said to her, "Do not weep." And He came up and touched the coffin; and the bearers came to a halt. And He said, "Young man, I say to you, arise!" The dead man sat up and began to speak. And Jesus gave him back to his mother. Fear gripped them all... .[20]

> "Ultimately, the problem of the meaning of history revolves around the question: 'Who is man himself and what is his origin and final destination?' Outside the central biblical revelation of creation, the fall into sin and redemption through Jesus Christ, no real answer is to be found to this question..."
>
> Herman Dooyerweerd, Dutch professor of philosophy

Fear indeed. Had I been present when the young man sat up in his coffin, I would have needed a place to sit down! Jesus had compassion for the widow, and raised her son from the dead. Many others present that day had compassion, too, but all they could do was weep. The gulf between the two is immense. The only way this incident would not revolutionize every person's view of Jesus is if they denied that it ever happened. But on what basis? These are the most reliable records of antiquity. The people who saw this miracle that day realized that Jesus was special as indicated by their comments that "A great prophet has arisen among us!" and "God has visited His people!" Joseph's boy never did things like *this* before. It was getting harder and harder for His contemporaries to refer to Him as only the carpenter's son. In the first chapter we realized that death is the ultimate victor of our life if the finite triangle is all there is. But Jesus demonstrated that if we trust in Him, the infinite and incarnate God, then for us death doesn't win any more.

Authority over Nature[21]

Jesus and His disciples were crossing the Sea of Galilee in a fishing boat typical of the day, equipped with sleeping and storage area under a deck covering, when a severe wind, familiar to Galilean fishermen even today, threatened their lives. In the midst of His disciples' panic, Jesus was awakened. He "rebuked the wind and the surging waves, and they stopped, and it became calm." As a scientist I am acquainted with the laws of nature. In Jesus we come face to face with the law-Maker. His mastery over natural elements was so instant and decisive, that those who were with Him appropriately asked, "Who then is this, that He commands even

Jerry Hawkes at www.holylandphotos.org
JESUS BOAT
Buried in the sand of the Sea of Galilee, this fishing boat dates to the time of Jesus and was undoubtedly similar (inset model) to those used by fishermen like Peter.

www.holylandphotos.org

the winds and the water, and they obey Him?" That is a very good question.

The incidents above are only four of the thirty-four miraculous events that the eyewitnesses of Jesus recorded in the Gospels. Could Jesus, were He a human teacher only, forgive sin against God, heal the physical body, raise the dead, and command nature to obey Him? Perhaps, some say, He was only like the prophet Elijah who, as a human, also did miraculous acts. But there was a significant difference between the two that would have been very evident, especially to the Jews of His day. It was characteristic of all the prophets to preface or conclude all they did with a "Thus says the Lord" or "Thus the Lord did." No prophet ever claimed the power to do a miracle outside of God. But Jesus said, "I am the Resurrection and the Life," "I give eternal life," and "I am the light of the world." If He were only a prophet, then He would have been a blasphemer and a liar.[22]

Many Other Convincing Proofs

It was Jesus' strategy to give reasons for people to believe His claim to be God. His invitation was clear: "Do not believe Me unless I do what My Father does. But if I do it, even though you do not believe Me, believe the miracles..."[23] That is what we have been looking at, i.e., the miracles of Jesus. In addition, as a result of recent study, I have noticed other indications of Jesus' deity in the historical records as well.

Acceptance of Worship[24]

Before Jesus began His public ministry, He experienced forty days of temptation in the wilderness. When He was invited to worship the devil in exchange for an earthly kingdom, Jesus quoted the Law, "You shall worship the Lord your God and serve Him only."[25] Later, during His ministry, His followers directed their worship toward Him, and He accepted it without any indication of protest. In fact, He approved of it. One has to conclude that Jesus was either a disgusting hypocrite or saw Himself as worthy to receive that which was reserved for God alone. On another occasion Jesus was receiving praise, and justified it by quoting an Old Testament Psalm stating that God had prepared such praise for Himself.[26]

Authority over Demonic Spirit Beings[27]

At the city of Capernaum Jesus was confronted by a demon-possessed man. Jesus rebuked the demons, "Be quiet and come out of him!" There was uncontested obedience. Who would have such authority? There are not many choices. The Jewish religious leaders realized this and on one occasion accused Jesus of being demonic Himself, thereby casting out demons by Beelzebul, the ruler of the demons. The other choice is that He has authority because He is God. The response of the people at Capernaum was, "What is this message?" or, what does this demonstrate to us about who He is? They recognized that such authority was evidence that He was more than a mere man.

Claim to be Sinless, the Only Way, and a Ransom for Mankind

The profile of Jesus that emerges from this sort of field trip into the historical records is often surprising to those who are skeptical. It was to me years ago when I doubted the truthfulness of the biblical accounts. While several of the observations that I have included above are the result of more recent research, the limited knowledge I did have forced me to rethink my position about Jesus. In addition to all the rest, Jesus made several statements that, if true, make Him unique. He claimed to be without sin: "Can any of you prove Me guilty of sin?"[28] He said that He was the exclusive way to God: "I am the way, and the truth, and the

A SUMMARY OF SELECTED ACTIONS OF JESUS		
1.	**He demonstrated authority to forgive sin** He forgave offenses that only God could forgive, and removed sin's temporal and eternal consequences.	Luke 5:17-26
2.	**He demonstrated power to raise the dead** He broke the bondage in which death held all people.	Luke 7:11-16
3.	**He demonstrated control over nature** He commanded and natural law obeyed.	Luke 8:22-25
4.	**He accepted worship from His followers** He accepted worship which He said was to be reserved for God alone (Luke 4:8).	Matthew 14:33; 28:17
5.	**He demonstrated mastery of demonic spirits** He commanded and the spirit world obeyed.	Luke 4:33-36
6.	**He lived a sinless life** No one was able to accuse Him of sin.	John 8:46
7.	**His life was uniquely valuable before God** He offered his life as a ransom to God for our forgiveness.	John 14:6 & Mark 10:45, with Psalm 49:7-9

Figure 2.

life; no one comes to the Father, but through Me."[29] And He stated that His life had such value as to redeem humankind to God, something no other human could do.[30] In view of all this, it is not surprising that Jesus caused such a revolution in the lives of His disciples.

IDENTIFYING THE LOGICAL OPTIONS

It is inevitable that anyone acquainted with the historical data concerning Jesus will have to face up to a decision concerning Him. Jesus, Himself, raised the critical question to those who had witnessed this evidence in person for more than two years. At a retreat near Caesarea Philippi, at the base of Mount Hermon, Jesus asked the disciples, "Who do you say I am?"[31] Though removed in time 2,000 years, the question is still extremely relevant. What would you say? What options do we have?

Jesus is a LEGEND

This view was popularized prior to the twentieth century and took on unmerited legitimacy only because the evidence that refutes it was yet unknown. The position was reasonable when it was thought that the New Testament records were late second-century writings. But with their early dating in the first century, within the lifetime of the eyewitnesses (as discussed in Chapter 2), this view is no longer tenable.

Jesus is a LIAR

Jesus claimed to be God and those who heard Him understood what He was saying. A logical examination of this claim could lead to three additional options concerning Him. First, either *He is* or *He is not* who He claims to be. Surveys continue to indicate that more than 90 percent of the people in this country believe there is a God or higher power. But if they were asked if Jesus is that God exclusively, many would be reluctant to go that far. It is common to hold the opinion that Jesus is only a wonderful man, a great moral teacher. But is this position logical in view of His claim to be God?

If Jesus claimed to be God and He is not who He claimed to be, then either *He knew it* or *He didn't know it*. Now if He claimed to be God, knowing that He wasn't, then He is a LIAR. He lied about Himself, and received worship as if He were God Almighty. If Jesus is a liar, then He has deceived more people than any other human, for the Christian movement that He began is the largest religion in the world. He could not be the greatest liar who ever lived, and also be a great moral teacher. Besides, He would be a fool, because He died for that lie. Was Jesus a liar? No, because His character throughout the historical accounts support a person of virtue and integrity. No, because it is inconceivable that Jesus could sustain a committed following for several years without being detected as a fraud. No, because He was authenticated by His resurrection from the dead.

Jesus is a LUNATIC

At first glance, the other option may seem more plausible, i.e., *He didn't know* He wasn't God. Jesus claimed to be God, was not, but really thought that He was. Could Jesus have been deluded? O. Quentin Hyder, practicing psychiatrist in New York City, analyzed the records of Jesus' behavior, personality and relationships for symptoms of psychiatric disorders. He concluded his study by pointing out that the evidence does not support the view that Jesus was a lunatic. Rather, He demonstrated qualities of excellent mental health.

A person is free to maintain that Jesus, out of honest delusion, made His claim to deity. But if one takes this position, he does so without any psychological evidence in its support and, indeed, in spite of considerable evidence to the contrary.[32]

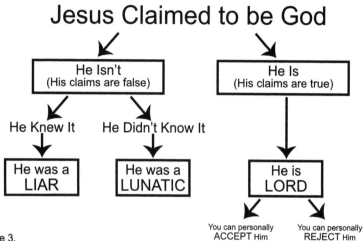

Figure 3.

Jesus is the LORD

Only one option remains. Jesus claimed to be God — and He is. He is the LORD. One final consideration carries a lot of weight to make this the option best supported by the evidence.

THE CRITICAL EVIDENCE: JESUS' RESURRECTION

Jesus promised several times during His three-and-one-half year ministry that He would rise from the dead.[33] Indeed, when asked by the Jews what evidence He would give to authenticate Himself, He said, "Destroy this temple, and in three days I will raise it up."[34] He was, in fact, speaking of His own body, i.e., His own physical resurrection. This would be the central test to determine whether He was authentic. It should be noted that *all* other founders of world religions, e.g., Buddha and Muhammad, died. People go to their grave sites to pay their respects. Christians don't do that, however, because Jesus is not in a grave—He's alive. No other religious figure known to man has ever provided convincing objective evidence that he had risen from the dead. I don't believe it is possible to imagine any greater credential to authenticate Jesus' claim to be deity than His resurrection. But did it really happen? Lord Darling, former Chief Justice of England and obviously trained to sift through the evidence, was satisfied that the resurrection was reasonably supported:

> The crux of the problem of whether Jesus was, or was not, what He proclaimed Himself to be, must surely depend upon the truth or otherwise of the resurrection. On that greatest point we are not merely asked to have faith. In its favour as a living truth there exists such overwhelming evidence, positive and negative, factual and circumstantial, that no intelligent jury in the world could fail to bring in a verdict that the resurrection story is true.[35]

What is this evidence that has persuaded people for centuries from all walks of life, even those who have skills honed to detect truth from error? There are three major arguments.

The Tomb of Jesus Was Empty

Even the disciples themselves were skeptical. They described the women's testimony that they had seen the resurrected Jesus as "nonsense."[36] After all, there was a sixteen-member Roman guard and a one-and-one-half ton stone with a Roman seal covering the entrance to the tomb. Disturbing it meant death at the hands of the guards or death to the guards who allowed it. Jesus' body was prepared for burial as a mummy with some seventy-five pounds of gummy spices inside strips of cloth.[37] The cloths were still in the tomb—but the body wasn't in them anymore.[38] Thomas said in effect that unless he saw the physical evidence of the nail prints in His hands, he would never believe it. Jesus showed them to him—and he believed.[39]

The Jewish authorities, who were in the best position to check out the facts, never attempted to refute the empty tomb, only tried to explain why it was empty.[40] Dr. Paul Maier, historian at Western Michigan University, sums up the current situation:

> Accordingly, if all the evidence is weighed carefully and fairly, it is indeed justifiable, according to the canons of historical research, to conclude that the tomb of Joseph of Arimathea, in which Jesus was buried, was actually empty on the morning of the first Easter. And no shred of evidence has yet been discovered in literary sources, epigraphy or archaeology that would disprove this statement.[41]

Jesus Appeared Physically to Many People After His Resurrection

The historical Gospels record ten distinct physical appearances by Jesus to people during the forty days after His death. He "appeared to Cephas [Peter], then to the twelve. After that He appeared to more than five hundred brethren at one time, most of whom remain until now, but some have fallen asleep..."[42] C.H. Dodd has commented, that "There can hardly be any purpose in mentioning the fact that most of the five hundred are still alive, unless Paul is saying, in effect, 'the witnesses are there to be questioned.'"[43] These were not hallucinations because they were too diverse as to times, places and personalities. Besides, hallucinations are not collective to 500 people, and the psychological condition of belief and expectation was lacking—the disciples were persuaded against their wills. And His appearances were not illusions or fantasies because He stood with them and said, "See My hands and My feet, that it is I Myself; touch Me and see, for a spirit does not have flesh and bones as you see that I have."[44] He also ate with them. [45]

Yet it is the testimony from negative sources that is especially convincing. Jesus appeared to His brother James, who had rejected Him during His public ministry, and James later became the leader of the Jerusalem church that proclaimed the resurrection.[46] The apostle Paul testified that it was the appearance of the resurrected Jesus to him when he was Saul of Tarsus, an enemy and persecutor of believers, that converted him.[47]

The Lives of the Disciples Were Transformed

It is a well-known fact that the disciples of Jesus abandoned and denied association with Him during His arrest, trial and crucifixion.[48] Their reason was fear for their own lives. Subsequently, the disciples had real experiences that they believed were literal appearances of the risen Jesus. They were transformed from scared men hiding in the Upper Room into bold proclaimers of His resurrection. They were even willing to die for their conviction. Indeed, all but one of the eleven remaining apostles died a martyr's death, yet none ever denied seeing Jesus alive after His death, not even to save their very lives. People will die for what they believe to be true, but none will die for what they know to be false. Gary Habermas, apologist and philosopher, a specialist on Christ's resurrection, has drawn an important conclusion: "The disciples' transformation shows that they really believed that Jesus rose from the dead and disproves the fraud (stolen body) theory both because of this change and

> *Make no mistake: if He rose at all it was His body; if the cells dissolution did not reverse, the molecules reknit, the amino acids rekindle, the Church will fall . . .*
>
> John Updike, *Seven Stanzas at Easter*

because liars do not make martyrs."[49] The Watergate political scandal in the United States during the mid-70s illustrates this point. Sophisticated lawyers, faced with the threat of a few years in prison, were unable and unwilling to maintain their fraudulent cover-up.

J.N.D. Anderson, former director of the Institute of Advanced Legal Studies at the University of London, rightly said that the resurrection is "either the supreme fact in history or it is a gigantic hoax..." and if it is true, then "to fail to adjust one's life to its implications means irreparable loss."[50]

A HIGHLY PROBABLE VERDICT

The reader must be the judge of the evidence. Is it reasonable to consider Jesus as a liar, a lunatic, or merely a wonderful moral teacher? Oxford professor C.S. Lewis did not think so:

I am trying here to prevent anyone saying the really foolish thing that people often say about Him: "I'm ready to accept Jesus as a great moral teacher, but I don't accept His claim to be God." That is the one thing we must not say. A man who was merely a man and said the sort of things Jesus said would not be a great moral teacher. He would either be a lunatic—on a level with a man who says he is a poached egg—or else he would be the Devil of Hell. You must make your choice. Either this man was, and is, the Son of God; or else a madman or something worse. You can shut Him up for a fool, you can spit at Him and kill Him as a demon or you can fall at His feet and call Him Lord and God. But let us not come with any patronizing nonsense about His being a great human teacher. He has not left that open to us. He did not intend to.[51]

Our imaginary field trip through the Gospel accounts, though far from exhaustive, did examine a broad sample of the available historical data. As much as anything from ancient times can be, I believe the evidence validates the claim that Jesus is the incarnation of the infinite, personal God. Dr. Edwin Yamauchi, eminent scholar and archaeologist, has testified that "the historical evidence has reinforced my commitment to Jesus Christ as the Son of God who loves us and died for us and was raised from the dead. It's that simple."[52]

The implications of this truth have the potential of significantly changing our view of life. The issues are more than academic, they are also moral. You are faced with the decision to accept or reject Him as Lord. You have the freedom to turn away. But the stakes are too high to take the matter lightly. Jesus said,

> *"But the intellectual case for Christianity became powerful to me after reading* Mere Christianity *[by C.S. Lewis]. At the end of the week I could not imagine how you could not believe in Jesus Christ."*
>
> Charles Colson, chairman of Prison Fellowship

"I am the resurrection and the life; he who believes in Me will live even if he dies, and everyone who lives and believes in Me will never die. Do you believe this?"[53]

—Focus & Discussion—

1. Why is it so significant to Christianity whether or not Jesus was God? Do you agree that whether Jesus actually was God is the most significant issue of Christianity's validity? Why or why not?

2. Eyewitnesses to Jesus reported that He had authority over demons, death, sickness and nature, and that He could forgive and remove the eternal consequence of sin. Why are these statements important for determining His identity?

3. Based on the evidence of Jesus' actions presented in this chapter, can you think of other options that could be attributed to Jesus other than the three listed (liar, lunatic, Lord)? If so, explain and discuss.

4. What changed the minds of Jesus' contemporaries, even of many skeptics, from unbelief to faith that Jesus was God? (See Thomas: John 20:24-28; Saul: Acts 9:1-20.) Discuss the role of evidence and reason as a basis for faith in Jesus.

5. How did the information in this chapter impact your own understanding of who Jesus is?

CHAPTER 4

CAN FAITH BE REASONABLE?

Identifying the Biblical Principles of Faith
Discovering the Life-Changing Dimensions of Faith

"My biggest problem had always been the intellectual reservations. I knew there was a God, but I could never see how man could have a personal relationship with Him."
Charles Colson, former special counsel
to President Richard Nixon

"What we do with what we know is what Christian knowing is all about."
Os Guinness, author

Recently I was talking with a woman whose conviction and desire was to follow Jesus. I will never forget her reason for hesitation. It had little to do with the intellectual concerns of purpose in life, the historical reliability of the Bible, or the deity of Jesus. On those issues she had been satisfied. Instead, her hesitation was really a fear, "Will it make me into a sap?"

CONTEMPORARY STEREOTYPES OF FAITH

The misunderstandings of religious faith run deep in our society. A middle school teacher asked one of the young students, "What do you think faith is?" Without even a pause, the answer was given, "That's believing what you know isn't true!" When a university student was asked the same question, he said that "faith is believing what you cannot know."

That is not an uncommon idea of faith—as though faith is a second- or third-best way of operating in life. Knowledge, by which is meant intellectual apprehension, is assumed to be the best way. If one cannot know, then the next best thing is just to believe anyway. The implication being that such a position is at best precarious, if not actually being stupid (a "sap").

Sometimes religious people earn labels such as "anti-intellectual" or "those weak enough to need a crutch." A religious group in Arkansas made national news when their alleged faith got them into trouble with the law. Claiming to have received a vision from Jesus Christ that He was returning to the earth very soon, in faith they quit their jobs, kept their children home from school, and waited. Eventually they lost their homes because they could not pay the mortgages. Social welfare officials placed their children in foster homes and back into schools. The parents presented a caricature of faith on the evening news in homes across America.

More recently, national news focused on a court case where parents were being tried for the death of their daughter. Of what crime were they allegedly guilty? They claimed to have "faith" that God was going to heal their daughter. Therefore, they refused any medical care for her. She died.

Can faith be reasonable? Most negative impressions of faith are generated in us by what we see in other people, such as the much-publicized sexual abuse scandals by clerics in the church. But such impressions may also be generated by the eccentric neighbor next door, a devoutly religious yet strange aunt, etc. Interestingly, none of these stereotypes is derived from a careful study of the Bible itself. We don't want a concept of faith derived from someone's bad example. Rather, we should seek to know the meaning of faith straight from the source. Therefore, we will study the Bible to identify the principles of faith. Only then can we know if faith is intended to be reasonable.

IDENTIFYING THE BIBLICAL PRINCIPLES OF FAITH

The Essential Components

Sometimes there is confusion about the word "faith." Recently I asked some people to identify differences that may exist between the words "faith" and "believe." Several explained distinctions with considerable confidence. Yet, the fact is that in the Bible, "faith" is the noun and "believe" is the verb form of the same Greek word. They are interchangeable as illustrated in the familiar John 3:16: "For God so loved the world that He gave His one and only Son, that whoever believes [has faith] in Him shall not perish but have eternal life." There is no difference in meaning if the words in brackets are used in place of "believes." A close synonym that may also be substituted is "trust."

1. Knowledge

The university student who said that "faith is believing what you cannot know," would have quite a different impression if "trust" were substituted for "faith." Let me illustrate. "Do you trust so-and-so?" I ask, naming a person with whom he is not familiar. He would likely respond, "How can I trust him since I don't even know him!" "But," I would remind the student, "You said that 'faith (trust) is believing what you cannot know.' Now you say that you cannot trust (have faith) in someone if you do not know them. Which is correct?"

The apostle Paul leaves little doubt which one he thinks is correct. Writing to the people at Rome, he communicates an interesting and logical sequence.[1]

We must **call** on the Lord to be saved	➤	To call we must **believe** in Him	➤	To believe we must **hear** about Him	➤	To hear we must have someone **tell** us	➤	To tell they must be **sent** out

Figure 1.

The apostle then summarizes his teaching on faith: "Consequently, faith comes from hearing the message, and the message is heard through the word of Christ." The meaning is better stated as, "Belief, you see, can only come from hearing the message, and the message is the Word of [concerning] Christ."[2] According to the apostle, faith cannot even get started without knowledge. I don't believe in "nothing," I believe in "something." In other words, faith requires an object.

Faith is not the same as sincerity, nor does sincerity make faith genuine. Suppose that I was asked if I believed a certain chair could hold me. Since other people were sitting on similar chairs, and because the chair looked perfectly normal, I was confident that it would. Being impatient with further questioning on the matter, I exclaim emphatically, "I have no doubt in my mind the chair will hold me!" However, if someone slipped in earlier and cut the legs through so that the least touch would topple it, my confidence and sincerity would be of no avail. My faith is only as good as the object in which I place it. If the chair is good, my faith will be good. But if the chair is bad, no matter how sincere I am, I am destined for a fall and my faith is misplaced.

A tragic incident at a local hospital was reported in the media. A nurse connected a patient to an "oxygen" source, and he immediately died. The source was mislabeled. It was actually a poisonous gas. Was the nurse competent and sincere? Did she really believe the gas was oxygen? Yes, on every count. But she was sincerely wrong. The object of her faith was defective, thus her faith was in vain.

The significance of knowledge to a valid faith must be understood. The object of Christian faith is the person of Jesus. If He is not who He claims to be, the incarnate Son of God, then no amount of sincerity, confidence, or religious experience can make it legitimate. This is precisely the conclusion of the apostle Paul to the people at Corinth. He said that "if Christ has not been raised [from the dead], then our preaching is vain, your faith also is vain...your faith is worthless."[3]

There is an important application of this observation to comparative religions. Christians cannot claim superiority to other religions on the basis that Christians are more sincere or make more personal sacrifices in the living out of their faith. That may not be true. The point of distinction between religions is the object they are trusting for their life and eternity. The historical evidence demonstrating that Jesus is the genuine article — the Son of God — means (as He said Himself in John 14:6) that "there is salvation in no one else; for there is no other name under heaven that has been given among men, by which we must be saved."[4] The Christian mission, therefore, is not about judging the sincerity, morality or culture of other religions, but instead merely inviting people to transfer

> "No intelligent person desires to substitute prudent acceptance of the demonstrable for faith; but when I am told that it is precisely its immunity from proof which secures the Christian proclamation from the charge of being mythological, I reply that immunity from proof can 'secure' nothing whatever except immunity from proof, and call nonsense by its proper name."
>
> J.S. Bezzant, English theologian

their trust (faith) to a different and certain object—Jesus Christ.

This is why it is so critical for us to know whether the New Testament is an authentic and historically reliable source concerning Him. Without eyewitness testimony it would not be objectively possible to determine if Jesus was credible in His claims, and thereby a worthy object of faith.

The apostle Paul is right. I can only put my faith in Jesus if I know about Him. And only if that knowledge indicates reasonable certainty of His deity will my faith in Him be any good. I cannot even get started into the area of personal faith without using my mind and interacting with the evidence. This first component of faith as taught in the Bible is certainly more attractive than the anti-intellectual caricature that I had of faith as a college student.

2. Will

The famous tightrope walker, Blondin, crossed the 1,100 foot expanse of Niagara Falls, 160 feet above the raging waters, at least 21 different times. On one occasion he accomplished the amazing feat blindfolded, and on another while pushing a wheelbarrow, to the amazement of thousands of onlookers. Promoters of these events asked the public for volunteers who believed he could do it again — and would be willing to prove their conviction by allowing Blondin to carry them across on his back. Although most professed to believe he would successfully cross the gorge, none were willing to risk the crossing with him. Finally, his agent and manager agreed to trust his life into Blondin's care. He was safely delivered to the other side, clinging to the aerialist's shoulders.

Knowledge is one thing, but choosing to commit one's life to that knowledge is another matter. Likewise, knowledge of Jesus is indispensable to faith, but it is only the first component. I could know exhaustively the evidence supporting the life of Jesus, and have no faith at all. The second faith component involves our will. This is illustrated once again in Paul's letter to the people at Rome.

> But not all the Israelites accepted the good news. For Isaiah says, "Lord, who has believed our message?"...But I ask: Did they not hear? Of course they did... Again I ask, Did Israel not understand?... But concerning Israel He [God] says, "All day long I have held out My hands to a disobedient and obstinate people."[5]

The people of Israel had disobeyed God, i.e., they lacked faith to trust Him. Paul is questioning why that was so. He asks the question whether they knew what God wanted. If not, the reason for their lack of faith would be a lack of knowledge.

I had a similar experience with my sons. Upon leaving my home for the day, I gave instructions for them to mow the lawn. When I returned that evening I noted that either the grass had grown at an unprecedented rate in the last few hours or they had failed to do what I had asked. I strongly suspected the latter. I went to them and used a question familiar to every parent, "Didn't you hear me?" Did I really think that at the moment I had spoken my instructions to them that morning, that the physics of sound waves had failed? No, I was quite confident my voice had reached their ears, but I was giving them the benefit of the doubt with my question. It turned out they did not have a knowledge problem. They had a "will" problem — they didn't want to mow the lawn.

In the passage above, Paul uses the same approach. He also concludes that the Israelites' problem was not caused by a lack of knowledge, but due to disobedience and obstinacy, i.e., a "will" problem.

Several years ago my wife and I had a disagreement. I no longer remember the issue, but it occurred on a Sunday afternoon. I was right, and she was wrong, but she wouldn't admit it! About the time we were getting quite intense, the doorbell rang. Answering the door, I was greeted by some good friends from another city who had stopped by because they were in the area. The transformation that immediately took place in my wife and me would make metamorphosis from a worm to a butterfly pale in comparison! We were instantly congenial and pleasant. After our friends left, I reflected on what happened. What was it that changed us? The doorbell?

I was not that naive. The doorbell did not change us — we did. By a deliberate choice, an act of my will, I changed. Why didn't I change sooner? I certainly knew from seminars, books and experience that my obstinate behavior was inappropriate to maintain harmony in a marriage relationship. The reason I didn't change before the doorbell rang, though, was that I didn't want to! I was exercising my will.

Faith is like that. In spite of the knowledge concerning Jesus that we have gained, if we do not exercise our wills, we have all the faith we are ever going to have — none. Unless we make a choice concerning who Jesus is, there will be no faith. A consenting will is the second essential component of the Bible's definition of faith. And that is certainly more attractive than the caricature of faith as mere emotion that I had rejected years earlier.

3. Response

Faith is knowing the truth about Jesus, and being willing to accept Him. But one of Jesus' parables identifies another factor in faith: Faith is not the same as good intentions.

"What do you think? There was a man who had two sons, He went to the first and said, 'Son, go and work today in the vineyard.' 'I will not,' he answered, but later he changed his mind and went. Then the father went to the other son and said the same thing. He answered, 'I will, sir,' but he did not go. Which of the two did what his father wanted?" "The first," they answered. Jesus said to them, "I tell you the truth, the tax collectors and the prostitutes are entering the kingdom of God ahead of you. For John came to you to show you the way of righteousness, and you did not believe him, but the tax collectors and the prostitutes did. And even after you saw this, you did not repent and believe him."[6]

The point Jesus makes is that faith is proven by its action. If there is no response derived from the will and the knowledge, then there is no faith either. In other words, according to the teaching of the Bible, to

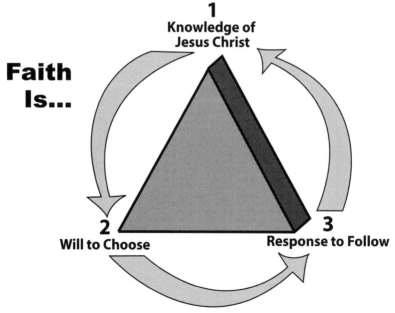

Figure 2.

qualify as legitimate, faith must consist of all three components: knowledge, will and response. Frequently, I talk with people who consider abandoning any further pursuit of truth, once they are satisfied intellectually and are no longer inclined negatively toward it. They want to walk away at that point without making any response. But response is concerned with the implications of the truth for my life. James, the brother of Jesus, is quite concerned with this third component of faith when he says that "faith by itself, if it is not accompanied by action, is dead."[7]

The three corners of a triangle (see Figure 2) can be used to represent the three essential components of biblical faith. Based on this diagram, faith is traveling the triangle. Jesus spoke a parable illustrating that there are really only two types of people; that is, those who travel the triangle and those who don't. The consequences in their lives are amazingly different:

Why do you call Me, "Lord, Lord," and do not do what I say? Everyone who comes to Me, and *hears* My words, and *acts* upon them, I will show you whom he is like; he is like a man building a house, who dug deep and laid a foundation upon the rock; and when a flood occured, the torrent burst against that house and could not shake it, because it had been well built. But the one who *has heard*, and *has not acted accordingly*, is like a man who built a house the ground without any foundation; and the torrent burst against it and immediately it collapsed, and the ruin of that house was great. [Emphasis added.][8]

The story is told of a fisherman with an enviable reputation — he always caught a large quantity of fish. But he also always fished alone. An elderly gentleman from a distant city, saying that he wanted to learn fishing as a retirement hobby, begged the fisherman to teach him the sport. He refused repeatedly but the persistent doggedness of the retiree finally broke him down. At the lake the elderly man was surprised that the great fisherman had only a metal box and a net for gear. Upon reaching a remote corner of the lake and leaving the motor running, the fisherman opened his metal box, pulled out some dynamite sticks, lit them, heaved them overboard and raced the other way with the boat. After the blast, he circled around and began netting the fish that had been stunned. The senior citizen had seen enough of this fishing method. He pulled his game warden badge from his pocket and flashed it before the fisherman. With but a momentary pause, the fisherman pulled out more dynamite, lit and thrust it into the game warden's hand with the comment, "Now, are you going to fish or are you just going to sit there!"

Faith is like that. I have heard people say that they wish they had someone else's faith. But often they have exactly the amount of faith that they are willing to have. They have not even responded to the knowledge they already had about Jesus.

The Resulting Definitions

It is usually helpful to attempt a definition of a subject to enhance communication. Rarely, however, have I encountered a definition of faith. Faith is easier to illustrate than define, but I have created two definitions that have helped me.

Head to Foot Commitment

The first is a homely one that derives from a brief anatomy lesson. (I always assume that every one's favorite subject in school was biology!) If we were asked to parallel the appropriate anatomical parts with the three points of the faith triangle, the head as knowledge, the heart as will, and the feet as response would be our likely choices. Consequently, we may define faith as "making a commitment to God from head to foot." At least it is simple! But had I heard such a definition when I was questioning everything in college, I would either have denied it as true or I would have had to rethink my caricatures.

I would never have imagined faith starting with the head, i.e., with reason, evidence and knowledge. This definition says that once the mind is satisfied, the process, figuratively speaking, moves to the heart where the will must interact with the data concerning Jesus. I imagined that people of faith were "no-minds" who acted on the basis of emotion alone. Finally, the definition, again figuratively, moves the process to the feet or the place where there is life response. The whole person is satisfied, and a new alignment or orientation to Jesus is established.

A Commitment-Making Process

The second definition is more descriptive: Faith is a commitment-making process, based upon the Word of God, and without regard to any emotional questioning of that Word.

...A Commitment-Making Process.

I find it helpful to apply the definition to starting a new business

> "Hell is God's great compliment to the reality of human freedom and the dignity of human choice."
>
> G.K. Chesterton, British writer

— a fast-food restaurant. I would want to begin with some market research on the eating preferences of people in the area, the number of competing businesses already operating, the availability of a building site, etc. The gathering of this critical information is equivalent to the "knowledge" component of the faith triangle. But I do not have a restaurant even if I have the most complete market research ever done. Eventually my interaction with the information must result in a choice whether or not to build. Even if my choice is affirmative, I still do not have a business. The knowledge and choice must be followed up with building, contracting with suppliers, hiring, and a variety of other responses that are consistent with the former two components. The commitment-making process that I have just described is analogous to traveling the faith triangle. I study the person of Jesus, make a confession of faith concerning Him, and then follow Him in obedience.

...Based upon the Word of God.

However, the definition does not stop there. It has two conditions to guide the commitment-making process. First, the source is to be the Word of God that we have analyzed for reliability in Chapter Two. It may also include evidence about Jesus discussed in Chapter Three. Finally, in the sense that the Word of God is seen as the truth of God, we may even include evidence in the natural world such as order and design. This is certainly superior to the ignorance, prejudice and deception that had shaped my earlier beliefs.

...Without Regard to any Emotional Questioning of that Word.

The second condition recognizes human emotion as a reality, but denies that it should determine the outcome of the commitment-making process of faith. Emotions are not always consistent with what is right — jealousy, lust, depression and insecurity being obvious examples. Furthermore, a faith commitment to follow Jesus may run counter to emotions that are linked to peer pressure, popularity and pride. Therefore, it is better to recognize that emotions add an in-depth, whole-person experience, but within the context defined by the Bible's teaching.

The Premier Example: Abraham

An incident in the life of the Old Testament patriarch Abraham will help to illustrate this definition of faith. Isaac was a miracle child for Abraham and Sarah. Born when they were very old, he was a child through whom God promised to give them descendents numerous "as the stars of the heavens" and "as the sand which is on the sea shore," and through whom "all the nations of the earth shall be blessed."[9] Isaac, born so late in his parents' lives, their only child, and the subject of such marvelous promises, was very dear to Abraham and Sarah.

Then the day came when God tested Abraham's faith: "Take now your son, your only son, whom you love, Isaac, and go to the land of Moriah; and offer him there as a burnt offering on one of the mountains of which I will tell you."[10] The thought is repulsive, but this event prefigured another one that would be the single, most important event in the history of humankind.

I could think of a lot of reasons to sleep late the next morning after hearing a message like that. But Abraham rose early to go — I suppose because he felt so good about it! No, but he chose (will) to be obedient (response) to the Word of God he had received (knowledge). The emotional questioning that undoubtedly flooded through him did not determine his response. But struggle he did. How could God fulfill the many promises that He made concerning Isaac if Isaac were dead? He knew that God is righteous and can not be unfaithful. By the time he arrived at the place of sacrifice three days later, he had resolved it in his mind: "Abraham reasoned that God could raise the dead..."[11]

TEMPLE MOUNT IN JERUSALEM   Dr. Carl Rasmussen at www.holylandphotos.org
The Temple Mount in Jerusalem (left of center, surrounded by wall) is identified with the ancient Mount Moriah in the incident with Abraham and Isaac recorded in Genesis.

As the altar was prepared on the mountain, Isaac asked a pertinent question, "...where is the lamb for the burnt offering?" Abraham hoped against hope when he said that "God Himself will provide the lamb for the burnt offering, my son." But it was Isaac who ended up on the altar. Not until Abraham raised the knife to slay his son did God cry out, "Do not lay a hand on the boy... Now I know that you fear God, because you have not withheld from Me your son, your only son." I'm sure that Abraham did not debate with God whether He was certain that He wanted to change His mind about Isaac! With great rejoicing that his son could live, he accepted a substitute sacrifice that God had indeed provided—a ram caught by its horns in a thicket. God *did* provide the lamb for the sacrifice, just as Abraham had told Isaac. Abraham was so grateful that he worshiped God using the name, *Jehovah-Jireh*, which in Hebrew means "The Lord Who Provides." This all took place on a mount called Moriah, which in Hebrew means "The Place of Provision." Put together it is "The Lord Who Provides in This Place."

It is natural to focus on the intense human elements of this event, while knowing nothing of its greater significance. Most would think that the event has no relevance for our lives today, but that is a serious over-sight. The "land of Moriah" where this event took place about 2000 B.C., is now known to be the area of Judea around Jerusalem. In actual fact, it is the hill or temple mount on which the Jewish temple was later built that was known as Mount Moriah.[12] It is the same hill that Abraham 2,000 years earlier had referred to as "The Place of Provision," and where the Jews in Jesus' day sacrificed many lambs as the atonement for their sin, according to Mosaic Law. When Jesus first began His public ministry, He was introduced by John the Baptist as "the Lamb of God, who takes away the sin of the world!"[13] It was at the temple that God offered His only Son Jesus to die so that many children of Abraham could live, i.e., "to those who are of the faith of Abraham." The lamb that God provided to spare Abraham's son physically, foreshadowed the Lamb (Jesus) that God provided 2,000 years later on the same hillside so that Abraham's de-scendents by faith could live spiritually and eternally. The Lord truly did provide for us in that place.

Consider Abraham: "He believed God, and it was credited to him as righteousness." Understand, then, that those who believe are children of Abraham. The Scripture foresaw that God would justify the Gentiles by faith, and announced the Gospel in advance to Abraham: "All nations will be blessed through you." So those who have faith are blessed along with Abraham, the man of faith.[14]

Therefore, the promise comes... by grace... for us who believe in Him who raised Jesus our Lord from the dead. He was delivered over to death for our sins and was raised to life for our justification.[15]

It is hard to imagine that this is all just coincidence. The "seed" [singular] of Abraham, i.e., Jesus Christ, has made possible spiritual descendents of Abraham all over the world who number as the stars and sand grains, a blessing to every nation on the earth, including the Gentiles (non-Jews). If we trust Jesus as our Savior and Lord, then we are some of those descendents of Abraham through our faith—"stars" and "sand grains" that God promised Abraham about 4,000 years ago.

DISCOVERING THE LIFE-CHANGING DIMENSIONS OF FAITH

Even if I had known about the three components and the definitions of faith (the biblical principles) during my search for answers as a young man, I don't think I would have responded to it. It would have helped remove some of the vagueness of the concept that was in my mind. But there was still a big question about faith that bothered me a lot: I wasn't sure I would be able to keep it up. At that time I viewed being a Christian as following a set of behavioral rules and regulations. I despised hypocrites, and I certainly didn't want to be one. Later I realized that my concern stemmed from a critical misunderstanding of how a person becomes a Christian.

A New Relationship: The GIFT of God's Presence

I viewed faith as a human enterprise — choosing a set of spiritual guidelines to follow. The focus was on how well I might be able to match my life to the rules. The day came when I discovered that faith was a relationship — with God. Since that time my study and experience have confirmed that truth. The discussion that follows is the way I would explain the life-changing dimensions of faith today.

Jesus, at the autumn Feast of Tabernacles in Jerusalem, focused attention on this matter:

On the last and greatest day of the Feast, Jesus stood and said in a loud voice. "If anyone is thirsty, let him come to Me and drink.

Whoever believes in Me, as the Scripture has said, streams of living water will flow from within him." By this He meant the Spirit whom those who believed in Him were later to receive.[16]

It is obvious that Jesus was referring to something supernatural — the Spirit of God within a person. How could this be? The naturalistic presuppositions of my scientific training had caused me to view such an idea with incredulity. But there is no mistaking the teaching. The night before His crucifixion, Jesus told His disciples that after He ascended they would receive another Counselor, the Spirit of truth, who "will be in you."[17] The apostle Paul affirms this, too: "Do you not know that your body is a temple of the Holy Spirit, who is in you, whom you have received from God?"[18]

How and when does this happen? Paul explains in his letter to the believers in Ephesus: "And you also were included in Christ when you heard the word of truth, the Gospel of your salvation. Having believed, you were marked in Him with a seal, the promised Holy Spirit, who is a deposit guaranteeing our inheritance..."[19] The "seal" is a mark of authenticity — that the believer really is a member of the family of God. The "deposit" is an earnest or token of what is to come, signifying that God will never abandon His followers in this life, and assures fulfillment of His promise to give them eternal life after death.

This adds a relational dimension to the faith triangle. When we travel the triangle, thereby trusting in Jesus Christ as the object of faith, we receive the divine person of the Holy Spirit to live within us. The teaching that the Christian faith is more than a moral code to live by is indispensable to one's understanding of its dynamic nature.

That is why Jesus was so direct when He spoke to Nicodemus, a representative of the very religious Pharisaic party.[20] Nicodemus lived by a high ethic, a moral man. But Jesus told him he was not going to heaven ("enter the kingdom") on that basis alone. Rather, he must be "born of the Spirit." Literally, the expression "born again" means to be given new life from above. Many people that I talk to think that they will go to heaven because they have cleaned up their act or have gone straight. It is something they can pull off if they try hard

> "It is not a mere acceptance of certain beliefs and dogmas, though they are necessary, but essentially it is living in close fellowship with Christ. It is not only a religion to be practiced, but also a life to be lived."
>
> Bishop John A. Subhan
> (convert from Islam)

84

enough. But this is not so. Jesus said we become Christians when God does a miracle of spiritual conception within us as we respond in faith to Him. The result is a faith in which we experience the gift of God's presence changing us within instead of one that controls us by an external code of do's and don'ts.

A New Freedom: The GIFT of God's Grace

So, as a young person, I had completely misunderstood the nature of the Christian faith. I now know it is not so much a religion as it is a relationship. Some reflection upon Jesus will help us to see why. Christians do not think of themselves as following the *teachings* of Jesus, but rather Jesus *Himself*. The reason is simple — Jesus is alive. You can find disciples of Muhammad or Gandhi but only in the sense that they try to live by the teachings these leaders left behind. Muhammad and Gandhi are dead. Their followers cannot have a personal relationship with them. In contrast, a Christian's faith is a relationship with the person of Jesus Christ who is very much alive, and whom he/she fully expects to see face to face.

This insight helps to erase a frequent misunderstanding, i.e., how to get and sustain faith. Some may understand me to be saying that faith is, first, exercising their will to affirm Jesus, and then, second, exerting a little discipline to order their lives according to His teachings. That is what people think who haven't looked seriously at what Jesus has to say. His example and teachings are relentless: "...love your enemies..."; "...every one who looks on a woman to lust for her has committed adultery with her already in his heart..."; "...no one of you can be My disciple who does not give up all his own possessions..."; forgive one another "seventy times seven" times; "...you are to be perfect..."!

After a few weeks or months of clenched fists and teeth gritted in sheer determination, a person will become exasperated trying on his or her own to conform to these standards. Bertrand Russell, British mathematician and philosopher, once said, "The Christian principle 'Love your enemies' is good,... except that it is too difficult for most of us..."[21] Trying to live like Jesus is not just difficult — it is impossible. Until we are shaken by the experience of our own moral ineptness, we will not appreciate the need for the gift of God's grace in our lives. We will also resist Jesus' analysis of our condition.

He [Jesus] went on: "What comes out of a man is what makes him 'unclean.' For from within, out of men's hearts, come evil thoughts, sexual immorality, theft, murder, adultery, greed, malice, deceit, lewdness, envy, slander, arrogance and folly. All these evils come from inside and make a man 'unclean.'"[22]

In the privacy of our own hearts and minds, we all know that what He said is true. As the British writer, G.K. Chesterton, said, the one doctrine of Christianity which is empirically verifiable is the fallenness of man.[23] Some may deny it, but our experience of trying to be really good only serves to remind us of the need for grace, i.e., unmerited favor. The apostle Paul explains: "For it is by grace you have been saved, through faith — and this not from yourselves, it is the gift of God — not by works, so that no one can boast."[24] Grace was necessary because we are morally inadequate before a holy God: "There is none righteous, not even one... no one who seeks God."[25] In fact, if you have an interest in God and are attracted to faith, it is not your own doing, for Jesus said that "No one can come to Me unless the Father who sent Me draws him."[26] One biblical passage in particular sums all this up quite clearly:

> But when the kindness and love of God our Savior appeared, He saved us, not because of righteous things we had done, but because of His mercy. He saved us through the washing of rebirth and renewal by the Holy Spirit... so that, having been

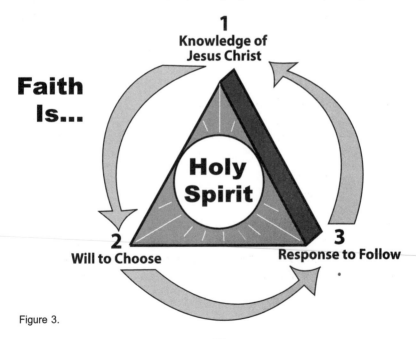

Figure 3.

justified by His grace, we might become heirs having the hope of eternal life.[27]

In view of these life-changing dimensions, the three corners of the triangle are no longer adequate to represent faith. The components are right, but we lack the desire and the power to do it. But what if the Holy Spirit Himself is placed at the center to create a supernatural dimension? For us even to be open to the evidence concerning the Bible and Jesus requires the convicting activity of the Holy Spirit. Twentieth-century theologian J. Gresham Machen described the process. "What the Holy Spirit does in the new birth is not to make a man a Christian regardless of the evidence, but on the contrary to clear away the mists from his eyes and enable him to attend to the evidence."[28] If, by His prompting, we respond and accept the gift of salvation through faith in Jesus Christ, the Holy Spirit takes up permanent residency within us. He transforms our fallen nature and desires from within, and provides the power to travel the triangle. As Paul says, "... [I]t is God who works in you to will and to act according to His good purpose."[29]

A New Hope: The GIFT of God's Heaven

The Christian faith promises a new relationship with the God who is really there. It also promises a new freedom from having to be good enough to earn God's approval. His grace means forgiveness, and new power and joy in life. But one preconceived fallacy about faith still remains.

I grew up thinking that no one in this life could ever know whether or not God had approved of them. That was a judgment only God could make after I died and the good and bad deeds had been tallied. I had to try as hard as I could and hope for the best.

It should now be apparent that this notion is inconsistent with the biblical principles of faith. How can one's destiny be uncertain if the object of faith, Jesus Christ, is certain? How can our deeds be the deciding factor if our relationship with God is a matter of grace? The apostle John sets the record straight:

God has given us eternal life, and this life is in His Son. He who has the Son has life; he who does not have the Son of God does not have life. I write these things to you who believe in the name of the Son of God so that you may know that you have eternal life.[30]

It is clear that God has already revealed the basis on which we can know who will go to heaven. In one of the most familiar passages in the Bible, He said that "whoever believes in Him [Jesus] shall not perish but have eternal life."[31] The apostle Paul said that "the gift of God is eternal life in Christ Jesus our Lord."[32] We can know right now that there is life after death, and that we will spend it eternally in heaven with God.

Testing Subjective Claims

Our testing of the claim that Jesus is God and the truth of the Christian faith began by looking only at the objective evidence of science and history. It is now obvious that there are also some very important subjective, experiential elements as well. Sometimes I am told that these subjective, anecdotal aspects don't really prove anything. Josh McDowell answers this challenge with an illustration.

> For example, let's say a student comes into the room and says, "Guys, I have a stewed tomato in my right tennis shoe. This tomato has changed my life. It has given me a peace and love and joy that I never experienced before..." It is hard to argue with a student like that if his life backs up what he says... A personal testimony is often a subjective argument for the reality of something.... There are two questions or tests I apply to a subjective experience. First, what is the objective reality for the subjective experience, and second, how many other people have had the same subjective experience from being related to the objective reality?[33]

When asked how he accounts for his life change, the student would answer, "A stewed tomato in my right tennis shoe." But to find even one other person in the entire world that has had a similar life change as a result of a stewed tomato in their right tennis shoe is improbable. The objective reality is more than a little suspect when it cannot be verified repeatedly in others.

When a Christian is asked for the objective reality that has resulted in a significant subjective life change, he/she would answer, "The person of Christ and His resurrection." How many others share this same result from a relationship with Jesus Christ? The evidence is overwhelming. There are millions of people from every nationality and profession that have experienced this kind of positive life change. Such broad confirmation greatly increases the validity of the subjective, life-changing dimensions of faith in Jesus.

Before Jesus left this earth He told His followers that He was going to prepare a place for them in heaven. He added: "And if I go and prepare a place for you, I will come back and take you to be with Me that you also may be where I am."[34] According to Jesus, the time is coming when every person that has ever lived will stand before Him. There is only one issue raised on that day of accounting: What did you decide to do about Him?[35]

It will be too late on that day to change your side—the choice will already have been made in life. It is the better wisdom to deal with this issue before then — to settle out of court! Then you can have assurance that the apostle Paul had: "Therefore, there is now no condemnation for those who are in Christ Jesus... [He] set me free from... sin and death."[36]

— Focus & Discussion —

1. Having learned about the three components of faith, explain how a person's commitment to follow Christ can be considered reasonable (based on an informed choice).

2. The point was made in this chapter that the Christian faith is reasonable. But suppose that a friend said to you, "If I had reasons, I wouldn't need faith." How would you answer?

3. Does including the third component ("Response") in the definition of faith support the unbiblical teaching that good works are necessary so you can earn heaven? Try to make a case for a "no" answer to this question.

4. Jesus taught that those who put their faith in Him would be given the presence of the Holy Spirit within them (John 7:37-39). Why is this necessary? Refer to the following Bible passages to assist in your response: Isaiah 59:2; John 8:34; Romans 3:22b-23; 5:12; 6:23a.

5. Do you think becoming a Christian is more of a reformation or a transformation? Which image is most appropriate to becoming a Christian: a) remodeling an old house (reformation), or b) metamorphosis of a caterpillar into a butterfly (transformation)?

6. Three life-changing dimensions of the Christian faith were identified in this chapter. Discuss how these life-changing dimensions about becoming a Christian are the same and different from your previous understanding. How do you respond to them: Excited? Skeptical? Accepting?

CHAPTER 5

WHERE AM I?

Analyzing Unbelief, Belief, and Doubt

"I thought it was very peculiar that I had acquired everything I had wanted as a child — wealth, fame and accomplishment in my career, I had beautiful children and a lifestyle that seemed terrific, and yet I was totally and miserably unhappy. I found it very frightening that one could acquire all these things and still be so miserable."
Racquel Welch, actress

❧

"The probability of life originating from accident is comparable to the probability of the unabridged dictionary resulting from an explosion in a printing factory."
Edwin Carlston, biologist at Princeton

S everal years ago my wife and I were doing a community survey of people's views concerning the Christian faith. A rather large, robust man came to the door at one home. When I asked him, "Would you be willing to answer some questions concerning faith?" he nearly exploded. The tirade that followed, accompanied by his anger, red face and bulging eyes, was frightening. Fortunately, my wife was there and I managed to hide behind her through most of it! Not wanting to leave on a sour note, we changed the subject to compliment him on his manicured lawn and beautiful flower beds. We hit a positive nerve. Being a yardsman myself, we engaged in a lively exchange of ideas and strategies. Before we left his home, I wanted to find out how to avoid a repeat performance of this encounter at the next house we visited. Had we done something to cause his ire?

He told us his story. At a previous residence he had lived alone except for a very special pet dog. He also had what he called a religious neighbor. On one occasion he let his dog out in the morning and was watching through the window. About the time the little dog was doing to the neighbor's shrubbery what dogs do to shrubbery, the neighbor stepped out of the bushes where he had been hiding and kicked the little dog nearly to the street. (Undoubtedly there was the religious neighbor's side of the story—which I was not hearing.) Because of internal injuries, the little dog had to be put to sleep. By this time the man is again red in the face and blurted out, "Now if that is what faith is like, I don't want any part of it!"

My first estimate of this man was that he was clearly a resolute unbeliever. After hearing his story, I knew that it was not that simple.

THE ANALYSIS OF UNBELIEF AND DOUBT

Could such unbelief as this man expressed be justified by the circumstances? Is this man's unbelief different from that of others who do not believe, but have no hostility at all? Where do the familiar spiritual doubts fit into the subject of faith? To have a more complete understanding of these matters, it is necessary to examine the counterparts of faith, namely unbelief and doubt. As a result, we will be able to determine more specifically in which position each of us stands.

The Nature of Unbelief

Over the years I have asked many groups of people to tell me what comes to their minds when they hear the word "unbelief." Typically, they produce the following one-word descriptions:

doubt	unsure	blind	rejection
unknowing	decision	wavering	rebellion
distrust	ignorance	indecision	arrogant
skepticism	willful	hard-hearted	

Even a casual examination of these words suggests that they do not represent a single concept. Indeed, there is quite a difference between "ignorance" and "rejection," and between "wavering" and "rebellion."

Are these diverse descriptions the result of surveying confused people, or are they honest attempts to communicate a complex subject?

Imagine with me that a lost tribe has just been discovered in the jungles of the Amazon. I volunteer to go to them so that I can share the historical facts concerning Jesus. Assuming language compatibility, our dialogue makes me acutely aware of the consequences of their years of isolation. They have never heard of any events of human civilization, much less the details about Jesus. They are in unbelief concerning Him; that is, they lack faith in Jesus. In this case there is a special reason for their unbelief — ignorance. Remember: How can they believe in what they have never heard? Knowledge is the first component necessary for faith. They do not know about Jesus, the object of Christian faith. Let's identify their condition as ignorant unbelief.

Now I spend every day, for several months, tirelessly telling these people about the basis for purpose and meaning, the historical and scientific evidence for the biblical writings, and what Jesus had said and done. After each session the people question and debate. Some are persuaded by a point or two, but wonder about others. They are back and forth over the issues, unable to establish a firm position concerning Jesus. They are still in unbelief, but for a different reason: they can't decide. The second component necessary for faith is an affirming will. They will need to make a choice about Jesus. Let us label their new condition as doubt.

Finally, after an additional period of teaching and questioning, the chief stands up to render his decision. To my horror it is now revealed that they are a cannibal tribe — there is a lot at stake here! The chief suggests to the others that I am "out to lunch." They reject the message concerning Jesus. They are in unbelief, but for a third reason: they have chosen not to believe. Let us express this condition as decisional unbelief.

The Forms of Unbelief

We are now able to make sense of the list of one-word descriptions of unbelief that people usually give. They identify three aspects of the complex nature of unbelief which can be categorized into the conditions through which the lost tribe progressed.

1. **IGNORANCE** — unknowing, blind

2. **DOUBT**— distrust, skepticism, unsure, wavering, indecision

3. **DECISION** — willful, hard-hearted, rejection, rebellion, arrogant

Unbelief exists in these three forms. The many words that come to people's minds when they think of unbelief are just synonyms of the basic three forms. The relationship between the forms is clarified by the diagram in Figure 1.

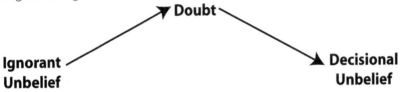

Figure 1.

The simplicity of determining the position we are in with regard to Jesus Christ should be apparent. I recall the time in my own life when I could no longer say that I didn't know enough about Jesus — that I was ignorant of the facts. Interestingly, in my own mind, I had not decided to reject Him either. Or had I? My first exposure to the evidences for the Bible and for faith had left me unsure and wavering, i.e., in doubt. I went through a necessary time of discrimination and hesitation before a firm position could be taken. But additional months of fact gathering did not change my indecision. I had already been persuaded that the evidence for Jesus' deity was excellent. Yet I remained in doubt and kept thinking that I needed to read one more book, check out one more fact, and so on, *ad infinitum*. Looking back on this time from my perspective today, I believe my skepticism had become, in reality, deliberate unbelief masquerading as doubt.

The Causes of Unbelief and Their Antidote

There are two primary blocks to a reasonable biblical faith. They are ignorance and willful rejection. The reason for this is evident when we recall the faith triangle. Knowledge concerning Jesus and an affirming will are the first two essential components of faith. When ignorance replaces knowledge and willful rejection replaces affirmation, there can be no faith.

If I were in ignorant unbelief, how could I get out of that condition? I would search for, be open to, and receive the readily-available information concerning the object of faith — Jesus. To illustrate this point, consider the five Christian missionary couples who were in South America attempting to tell the Auca Indian tribe about Jesus. The tribe was clearly in ignorant unbelief since the missionaries had not even met them yet, or understood their language. One day, while attempting to make personal contact, the five husbands were killed by the Aucas in a surprise attack. In spite of their tremendous grief over the loss of their husbands, the wives flew over the tribe and dropped gifts from their small airplane. This act of courage, love and forgiveness eventually won the opportunity for contact, and later, communication with the people. Ignorance concerning Jesus was removed by teaching the facts about His life. They later made a faith commitment to accept Jesus as their Savior. An incredible life change took place. In fact, the chief of the tribe later baptized the son of the missionary he had personally killed.[1]

What if I were in the unbelief position of doubt concerning Jesus? How could I move from that position? I must decide how much information is enough to give relative certainty about Jesus' identity, and to say either "yes" or "no" to Him as my Savior and Lord.

Finally, what would I do to get out of my position of decisional unbelief? Since this is a position of choice or decision, there is no other way out than choosing to reconsider my position. Thereby I would be returning to the "doubt" position, where I again examine the evidence to see if a "yes" to Jesus is not more reasonable and appropriate than a "no."

> "Contemporary unbelief does not rest on science as it did towards the close of the last century. It denies both science and religion. It is no longer the skepticism of reason in the presence of miracle. It is a passionate unbelief."
>
> Albert Camus, French writer

However, sometimes it is not that clear-cut. The two causes of unbelief, that is, ignorance and unwillingness, may be interrelated. The apostle Paul, speaking of certain unbelieving people, said that "They are darkened in their understanding and separated from the life of God because of the ignorance that is in them due to the hardening of their hearts."[2] It is disconcerting to think that if we fail to respond positively to what we know is true, a hardening of the heart may take place that immunizes us, so to speak, against hearing and accepting additional truth. We have already indicated above that we are free to harden our hearts and willfully say "no" to the knowledge of Jesus that we have. That remains our choice. Yet we now are forced to accept that our hard-heartedness may make us blind to truth — unable even to recognize it — by our very refusal to even listen or be open to the evidence at all. Furthermore, our stubborn wills may even attempt to rationalize the rightness of such an untenable position.

Sometimes I have wondered about the irate man whom my wife and I had called upon at his home. What form of unbelief was he in? My first impression was decisional unbelief. He appeared to be rebellious and hard-hearted. But after hearing his story, I changed my mind. I think he was in ignorant unbelief. He had rejected a caricature of faith, not the real thing. He seemed to know very little truth about Jesus at all. The concern I had for him was whether his anger over a foolish act by his so-called religious neighbor would forever shut him off from receiving the correct knowledge about Jesus that he needed to make a legitimate choice. Because of the stereotypes and caricatures of faith in society today, I have come to believe that ignorant unbelief, caused by a lack of familiarity with, or a refusal to listen to or be open to, the evidence, is the most common form of unbelief. In fact, this is the position from which the apostle Paul said he came as a former persecutor of Christians: "...yet I was shown mercy, because I acted ignorantly in unbelief..."[3]

The Analysis of Belief

The observation that we have free will results in the possibility of our saying "no" to the truth claim of the Christian faith. But to be truly free means that we may also choose to say "yes." This is the alternative to one of the unbelief positions, i.e., belief. Figure 2 indicates the positions we may be in, and the choices we are free to make.

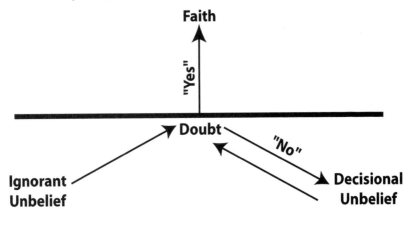

Figure 2.

The Operation of Belief

The idea that faith required a personal commitment became clear enough to me during my own search for certainty about God. What I did not understand at all, though, was the way in which faith was to operate in my life. Only later have I come to recognize that there is a counterfeit of faith which masquerades as the real thing. If the counterfeit is mistaken for the genuine, our faith in God can lead to disappointment and bitterness rather than fulfillment.

The Counterfeit: Contract Faith

There was a time in my life when I thought of faith in terms of a contract. The scenario went something like this: I was to believe that Jesus was the Son of God. In return, God would provide certain benefits for me — happiness, success, wealth and health — small things! This seemed only right in view of the sacrifice it was for me to conform my life to following Him. And I would continue to follow God as long as He lived up to His end of my imaginary contract. If He didn't come through to meet my expectations — well, forget it! In other words, this scenario describes a faith contract with conditions written in language such as "I'll believe if ..."

A classic example of this approach to faith is an incident in the life of Thomas, one of Jesus' disciples. Jesus had told His followers on several occasions that He would rise from the dead.[4] When Thomas was told by eyewitnesses that it had actually happened, he responded by saying, "Unless I see the nail marks in His hands and put my finger where the nails were, and put my hand into His side, I will not believe it."[5] One week later Thomas fell at Jesus' feet and exclaimed, "My Lord and my God!" Jesus then said to him: "Because you have seen Me you have believed; blessed are those who have not seen and yet have believed."

What was Thomas' problem? His alleged faith in Jesus was conditional — he insisted that he must physically see Jesus rather than believe the resurrection on the basis of what Jesus had promised beforehand. Thomas said, in effect, that he did not believe in Jesus because he would not trust His Word (nor the eyewitnesses), but would only believe if..., and expressed his conditions.

In rescuing the nation of Israel from slavery in Egypt, God demonstrated His faithfulness by overcoming impossible odds with many miracles. He then brought them to the land of Canaan and promised that He would take them in. Twelve men were sent into the country as spies for forty days, and returned with two reports.[6] The majority report of ten said that while the land was excellent, the inhabitants were giants and their cities strongly fortified. Thus, the people might as well head back to Egypt because there was no way for the land to be taken. What would change their minds? Perhaps if they had a dozen stealth bombers? — Or a battery of missiles? Their position was, "God, we would believe You can take us in, if..." Unfortunately, this is not faith at all—it is a counterfeit.

The Genuine: Surrender Faith

Contract faith, the counterfeit, is putting the onus on God to perform before we are willing to put our trust in Him. Actually, it is acting as though we were God and He must do our bidding. That is not exactly the appropriate attitude of a finite creature to the infinite Creator! We are the ones in need of God, not *vice versa*. We must come to God on God's terms, not on ours.

Furthermore, it implies that we don't think God can back up His Word, i.e., He isn't capable. But, if faith is as good as its object, and the object of Christian faith is the incarnate God, Jesus Christ, then whatever He says is the last word on any subject. Setting conditions is assuming that God has limitations. Surrender faith is not something I have to generate emotionally, or a confidence placed in a church. Surrender faith trusts unconditionally the infinitely powerful, wise, loving and just God who created and sustains all that exists. What He says, He can and does do. If we know God that way, then the "commitment-making process based on the Word of God" is a very reasonable way to live. Instead of "I'll believe if..." it is rather, "I believe God, period."

The counterfeit and genuine faith mentalities are illustrated by the Israeli spies. The majority reported that, despite God's command and promise, a successful invasion of Palestine was not possible. The minority report of the remaining two spies, Joshua and Caleb, stated that since God had instructed them to take the land, they should proceed immediately to do so. What is the difference? Joshua and Caleb were basing their recommended action on a powerful and faithful God Who had promised this land to them. No conditions could outweigh this single factor. But not so with the rest of the people. By following the majority report, they were indicating that other factors were more important in their consideration than God's Word. If those factors changed, then okay. Theirs was a contract with conditions, a counterfeit for faith. God's response to them underscores this point: "How long will these people treat Me with contempt? How long will they refuse to believe in Me, in spite of all the miraculous signs I have performed among them?"[7] The result was forty years of wilderness wanderings until Joshua and Caleb led the next generation into the promised land. The counterfeit of faith does not lead to relationship and fulfillment, but rather to disappointment and even unnecessary suffering.

The Illustration of Belief

The Roman Centurion

A Roman soldier made a statement which prompted Jesus to say to the multitude that followed Him: "I say to you, not even in Israel have I found such great faith."[8] What was there about the Centurion's faith which produced such glowing praise from Jesus?

The Centurion was a military officer who clearly understood authority. He had a favorite servant who was very sick and about to die. There is no indication that he had ever personally seen Jesus perform any miracles. Undoubtedly, he had heard stories of how Jesus had healed the sick, and sent some Jewish friends to ask Him to come. When Jesus drew close to his home, the Centurion sent a message, "Lord, do not trouble yourself further, for I am not fit for You to come under my roof; for this reason I did not even consider myself worthy to come to You, but just say the word, and my servant will be healed."

The Centurion, humbling himself, expected Jesus to be able to heal his servant, even from a distance, thereby acknowledging His position of absolute authority over disease. He interjected no conditions. Rather, he simply asked Jesus to issue the command. This unconditional faith in the person of Jesus was really the recognition of His authority as deity, and prompted Jesus to commend him in glowing terms. The servant was healed and restored to good health.

Noah

There was a time when God grieved that He had made humankind.[9] But one man knew and served God — and "found favor in the eyes of the Lord." Noah was to be saved from God's judgment by riding out the coming flood in an ark. It must be remembered that Noah did not live on the seaboard. He didn't even have a lakeside cabin. We can only imagine the scenario as God informed Noah of the coming deluge.

When instructed by God to build an ark, Noah probably wondered why he needed a boat where he lived. He had never needed one before. Never mind that — what kind of boat should it be? God gave additional details: make it 450 feet long, 75 feet wide and 45 feet high, with three decks. Noah may have gasped, though he did have a couple spare weekends coming up. Actually, from the time of God's instructions to the time of the flood was a period of 120 years. Noah worked to build this ship for 120 years. This gives new meaning to the concept of an avocation!

But, it may be recalled, he did have three sons to help him. A study of the text, however, reveals that the first son, Shem, was born about twelve years after the command to build. I can imagine how the family got started. After eleven years of very slow progress on the ark, Noah came home discouraged. He commented to his wife that he didn't think he would ever finish building it. But, together, they hit upon a great idea — Shem. Two more good ideas quickly followed, i.e., Ham and Japheth. Now there were five who could work on the project.

It is a curiosity to wonder how Noah handled being a public spectacle in the community. This was not exactly an inconspicuous canoe. He couldn't hide it behind a bush. There was no escaping the fact that he was building a massive ship hundreds of miles from the nearest large body of water. It was probably with some regularity that the boys questioned Noah, "Dad, are you sure that you heard that message right?"

The point is that Noah's decision to build the ark was made strictly upon his acceptance of God, and, thereby the authority of His Word. For 120 years he was probably made the brunt of every joke for miles around. If I had been in his situation, I probably would have asked for a sign to keep up the faith (one-half inch of rain per day would have been encouraging). But not Noah: "Thus Noah did; according to all that God had commanded him, so he did."

By faith Noah, being warned by God about things not yet seen, in reverence prepared an ark for the salvation of his household... and became an heir of the righteousness which is according to faith.[10]

By the time the ark was finished, it had already begun to rain. Water began to appear where it had never been before. The fool, Noah, began to look like a genius. His formula was really quite simple — he believed God unconditionally.

THE RESULTING IMPLICATIONS

Where Am I?

At times during my quest for spiritual certainty, I would end up thinking much like an agnostic. Maybe there were answers, but perhaps not — one could never know for sure. Faith is a personal thing, I thought — what works for some may not work for everyone. Reflecting upon those years from my current perspective, I believe this thinking stemmed from the ambiguity in my understanding. I had no clear distinction between the forms of unbelief, nor did I understand genuine versus counterfeit responses to God. If I had seen my options as I do now, I think I would have had a clearer focus and direction.

As I see it now, the first and central issue continues to be, "What position are we to take in regard to Jesus Christ?" Our response to this question alone determines whether we are in the "unbelief" or "belief" section of Figure 3.

Have I placed my faith in Jesus Christ alone for my salvation?

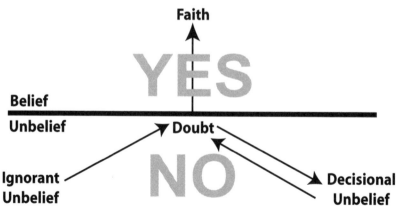

Figure 3.

Our discussion of the faith triangle in Chapter Four made clear the basic reasons why our response may be "no."

1. Lack of Knowledge (ignorant unbelief): I do not know what Jesus said and did, or the reasons for faith in Him.

2. Indecision (doubt): I have questions and emotional uncertainty about what choice to make.

3. Willful Rejection (decisional unbelief): I deny that Jesus needed to die for me, and I do not want to live for Him.

On the other hand, to respond "yes" would mean that we agree with the apostle Peter who said that "Christ died for sins once for all, the righteous for the unrighteous, to bring you to God."[11] It also would mean that we do what the apostle Paul said, that "...if you confess with your mouth, Jesus as Lord, and believe in your heart that God raised Him from the dead, you will be saved."[12] The apostle John tells us what will result: "...to all who received Him, to those who believed in His name, He gave the right to become children of God..."[13]

But even if we say "yes," we might view this faith relationship either as a contract with conditions, or as an unconditional surrender to God.

1. The Counterfeit: Contract "Faith": I give my life to God on the condition that He rewards me with health, wealth, heaven, etc. I have rights, make demands of God, and do good deeds to earn God's acceptance and special blessing.

2. The Genuine: Surrender Faith: I surrender my life unconditionally to God with repentance. I am accepted by His unconditional love and grace alone. I am motivated to do good deeds because of my love for Him, and enabled to do so by the inner power of the Holy Spirit.

In his book, *The Screwtape Letters*, C.S. Lewis creates a series of letters from Screwtape, a professional devil and under-secretary of the department of temptation, to his nephew Wormwood, a junior tempter. Commenting on the greatest threat to the efforts of the devil in a human's life, Screwtape writes:

Do not be deceived, Wormwood, our cause is never more in danger than when a human, no longer desiring, but still intending, to do our Enemy's will, looks around upon a universe from which every trace of Him seems to have vanished, and asks why he has been forsaken, and still obeys.[14]

This genuine faith is a trust that results from surrender to God because it has been persuaded by the evidence of who He is. It is not conditional on circumstances. Screwtape's description fits Jesus perfectly as He hung on the cross. He was not a victim — He chose to be there.[15] And when circumstances turned dark, He still stayed there.[16]

What Difference Does It Make?

We have seen that the Christian faith is reasonable. The evidence for God seen through the life of Jesus is conclusive. And if it is true, we should believe in Him because of who He is, not for any rewards or benefits that may come to us. But if He is real, then His presence in our lives has to make a difference. What does He promise as a result of a genuine faith relationship with Him?

> "It is because...the religious view of the universe [in its Christian version] seems to me to cover more of the facts of experience than any other that I have been gradually led to embrace it..."
>
> C.E.M. Joad, The Recovery of Belief

First, if I am in right relationship with God, then I am able to realize my human potential, i.e., become all that I was intended to be in this life. After all, if I want to know how a product can best be used, I go back to the manufacturer's instructions. Likewise, if God is my Creator, His specifications for my life should result in functional wholeness — intellectual, moral and emotional completeness. Jesus said, "I have come that they may have life, and have it to the full."[17]

Second, if I am in right relationship with God, then I am able to realize my eternal destiny, i.e., assurance of life after death. Jesus said, "Let not your heart be troubled; believe ... in Me. In My Father's house are many dwelling places; ...I go to prepare a place for you ... I will come again, and receive you to Myself; that where I am, there you may be also."[18]

Do we dare believe that Jesus is alive, coming to earth again in the future, and will take us to live in His presence forever? The apostle Peter warned there would be scoffers who say, "Where is this 'coming' He promised? Ever since our fathers died, everything goes on as it has since the beginning of creation."[19] He then reminds his readers that the people of Noah's day scoffed in the same way. But when the flood came, Noah looked like a genius — because he believed God, and lived by His Word.

Peter adds: "By the same word the present heavens and earth are reserved for fire, being kept for the day of judgment..." Why is Jesus so slow in keeping His promise to return? "He is patient with you, not wanting anyone to perish, but everyone to come to repentance."

I remember coming to the point in my life when I realized that I no longer had any major intellectual reasons keeping me from faith in Christ. But the effect of that realization was not what I expected. Instead of being eager to take that step, I was still holding back, being cautious. What was keeping me from letting go and allowing Jesus Christ to be in control of my life? Later I came to realize what it was — something very powerful and at the same time subtle. Only God was adequate to overcome the single most important factor that kept me from faith in Jesus Christ. But when He did, I was surprised.

— Focus & Discussion —

1. Which of the three forms of unbelief do you think is the most common? How might your answer vary for people in other countries of the world?

2. Assuming you were honestly seeking personal faith in Jesus Christ, is it important to know which form of unbelief you hold? Why?

3. Is it possible to mentally misjudge a person's unbelief or faith position based only upon first impressions? What is necessary to know for sure? What does this suggest about the importance of developing trusting relationships as a basis for discussing one's faith?

4. Sometimes we hear the expression, "Seeing is believing." Read 2 Peter 3:3-10. If a person followed the expression above, when would he/she believe in the second coming of Jesus Christ? What basis do Christians have for believing in the second coming of Jesus if not according to the expression above?

CHAPTER 6

HOW CAN I KNOW GOD?

Recognizing the Stumbling Block
Taking the First Step

"It's Jesus. It's Jesus that changed my life.
I want everyone to know it's Jesus."
The late Payne Stewart, professional golfer, to Pastor J.B. Collingsworth, after
watching video from Stewart's 1999 U.S. Open victory.[1]

෨

"Only God changes hearts."
Paul Azinger, professional golfer, discussing the conversion of his friend,
Payne Stewart

෨

"You and I have a God-shaped vacuum at the center of our being."
Blaise Pascal, seventeenth century French physicist

Several years ago I served as the academic dean of a small, Midwestern college. It was my job to interview candidates for faculty positions. I recall one candidate who was extremely likeable, but with limited education. I enjoyed his visit to our campus immensely, but knew I had to tell him that he was not qualified for the job. After what seemed like an hour of oblique comments and nuances in my attempt to be diplomatic, the man looked at me and asked, "What's the bottom line?" In one sentence, in about five seconds, I then told him the unguarded truth.

A student who had attended one of my college classes called me unexpectedly from his home during the summer break. After exchanging greetings, he talked at great length about an opportunity that was open to him. He was very complimentary to me about what a wonderful person and professor I was. Finally, I had to ask, "What is the bottom line? Why are you calling?" He then admitted that he wanted $1,500 from me.

Years earlier, something similar to this had happened to me in my quest for God. I had spent many months interacting with numerous lines of excellent evidence. I had dialogued with several people. I weighed the pros and cons of a commitment to follow Jesus Christ. But the time came when I had to ask the question, "What is the spiritual bottom line?" That question made me face up to the truth: It was no longer a series of legitimate intellectual questions that kept me from faith. I had to deal with something much more difficult — a spiritual principle inherent in the depths of my nature.

IDENTIFYING THE SPIRITUAL PRINCIPLE

The basic principle can be identified in an incident that occurred to Peter, before he became a believer and apostle.

One day as Jesus was standing by the Lake of Gennesaret, with the people crowding around Him and listening to the Word of God, He saw at the water's edge two boats, left there by the fishermen, who were washing their nets. He got into one of the boats, the one belonging to Simon, and asked him to put out a little from shore. Then He sat down and taught the people from the boat.

When He had finished speaking, He said to Simon, "Put out into deep water, and let down the nets for a catch."

Simon answered, "Master, we've worked hard all night and haven't caught anything. But because you say so, I will let down the nets."

When they had done so, they caught such a large number of fish that their nets began to break. So they signaled their partners in the other boat to come and help them, and they came and filled both boats so full that they began to sink.

When Simon Peter saw this, he fell at Jesus' knees and said, "Go away from me, Lord; I am a sinful man!" For he and all his companions were astonished at the catch of fish they had taken...[2]

The Prerequisite to Faith

After fishing all night and catching nothing, Peter and his crew were washing the nets and probably eager to get some rest. Fishing was no weekend sport for Peter, but rather his vocation. He was experienced and surely knew in detail every feature of the lake. He had undoubtedly tried every technique he knew that night. The fish just were not biting, so to speak. He was probably disgusted and not in a very good mood.

In this setting, Jesus, the carpenter and itinerant religious teacher (and novice fisherman!), suggests dropping the nets in deep water. The event that follows is most instructive. Peter is clearly reluctant because he is confident he knows exactly what will happen (and besides catching no fish, it will mean washing the nets again). To avoid embarrassment with his crew, he makes certain they know that this is not his idea ("because you say so"). Peter thinks he knows better than Jesus. This is his turf. On the beach, Peter is the "pro." Anyway, what does a traveling rabbi know about fishing? From this perspective, Peter addresses Jesus as "Master" or teacher, a title of respect but recognizing only His humanity.

Then comes the astounding, massive catch of fish. Peter's response is so significant. He now identifies himself as a "sinful man" and addresses

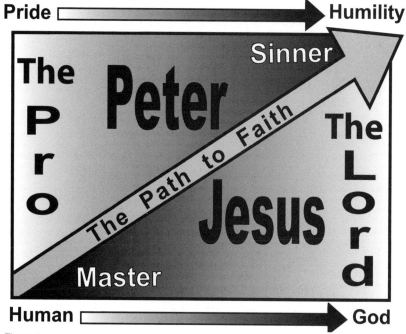

Figure 1.

Jesus as "Lord," meaning supreme in authority. The word he chose was "kurios," sometimes meaning simply "sir," but in most cases it is the translation of the Hebrew "Jehovah" or God. In view of Peter's sudden humility and his response of worship, it is clear that he is attributing deity to Jesus.[3]

The spiritual principle can be seen more clearly by referring to Figure 1. The upper and lower triangles within the rectangle represent Peter and Jesus, respectively. Before the miracle catch of fish, Peter is the "pro" and imagines that he knows more than Jesus (illustrated by the large base of his triangle on the far left). As the incident unfolds, illustrated by the "path to faith" diagonal from left to right, the upper triangle representing Peter becomes smaller, and the lower triangle representing Jesus becomes larger (illustrated by the large base of His triangle on the far right). The miracle revealed Peter's limitations and prideful independence. The result was his admission of sin and confession that Jesus is Lord. It was Peter's realization that Jesus is Lord that moved him from pride to humility. This insight and brokenness often occurs along the path to a faith relationship with Jesus.

The Key to Usefulness

The illustration in Figure 1 has clear implications for our lives. Intellectually, we may be persuaded by the evidence that Jesus is the incarnation of God. But our self-sufficiency and pride may keep us from acknowledging that we need Him. As long as we believe that we are the "pro," we will be unwilling to submit to Jesus' right as Lord to direct our lives. As Jesus said to the self-righteous and proud Pharisees, "It is not the healthy who need a doctor, but the sick. I have not come to call the righteous, but sinners to repentance."[4]

In my own case, humility was not my strong suit. My pride was the greatest deterrent that had kept me from faith and dependence on Jesus. In order to follow Him in obedience, I needed to experience His forgiveness and submit my life to be dependent on the power given to me by His Spirit.

ILLUSTRATING THE SPIRITUAL PRINCIPLE

It may be helpful to illustrate how this spiritual principle was reflected in the lives of John the Baptist and Moses, two people used by God in very significant roles.

John the Baptist

John the Baptist was six months older than Jesus and had lived a life of personal denial and singleness of mind. His whole life was a preparation to announce the coming of Jesus the Messiah, "the Lamb of God who takes away the sin of the world."[5] He had many disciples of his own, and a significant popularity. He had made great sacrifices for the success he was experiencing. It was easy for me to imagine him aggressively defending his right to his position and fame.

A few months later, John's followers came to him with an understandable concern: More people were beginning to follow Jesus than John. His followers had obviously become jealous and viewed Jesus' activities as an infringement on the rights of John. But John saw it differently. He testified, "After me comes a Man who has a higher rank than I, for He existed before me ... the thong of whose sandal I am not worthy to untie."[6] In total humility he then declared, "A man can receive nothing, unless it has been given him from heaven ... He must increase, but I must decrease."[7]

How could John do it? Because he was in a faith relationship with God and knew that doing God's eternal will was more important than temporal position and success. In other words, he had learned humility. Such an attitude was eulogized by Jesus as He later spoke of John: "I tell you, among those born of women there is no one greater than John."[8] It would have been difficult for me in my college years to imagine my competitive nature being controlled and channeled in such a humble way.

Moses

Everyone who is acquainted with the feats of Moses in Egypt would view him as a giant among men. But few realize that his reputation is based entirely on the period in his life after he reached eighty years of age. In fact, as I will attempt to demonstrate, the operation of the spiritual principle identified above in his early life was the key to his later greatness.

Moses was born the son of slave parents in Egypt at a time when the Pharaoh had declared a death sentence on male Hebrew newborns.[9] In a desperate move to save his life, his mother placed him in a basket in some reeds near the bank of the Nile behind the royal palace. Upon finding the crying child, Pharaoh's daughter felt pity and adopted Moses as her own son. It was by these providential circumstances that Moses enjoyed the luxury and privilege of royalty for the first forty years of his life. He is described as being "educated in all the wisdom of the Egyptians and was powerful in speech and action." Without exception, he was the most educated and powerful Jew in the world of his day.

At about the age of forty, Moses committed treason by killing an Egyptian guard out of sympathy for a Hebrew slave who was being beaten. He also attempted to be an arbitrator or judge in Hebrew disputes. The significance of these activities is found in Moses' perception of himself: "...he supposed that his brethren understood that God was granting them deliverance through him."[10] There is no biblical statement or even a hint that God had approached Moses to be His chosen deliverer at this time. God did approach him for this task forty years later — a critical delay for a very important reason.

It seems apparent that Moses had acted on his own. Why? He was the "big man" in the palace! However well intended, it is clear that he overestimated his own importance and impeccability. He was above the law, a benevolent autocrat. He was the "pro." Moses' pride led him to believe that if ever there was someone who had the power to save the Hebrews from their slavery, he was that person. But he was rebuffed by his own people, and to add insult to injury, his adopted Egyptian family pronounced a death sentence upon him. He had failed utterly, and ran for his life into the desert of modern Saudi Arabia, near the Gulf of Aqaba.

No competent vocational counselor would ever suggest a career of shepherding in the wilderness to the most educated and capable Jew in the world. Only God could know how remedial a forty-year stint in the desert would be to a bad case of self-sufficiency and pride. I can imagine how often Moses must have reflected on his failure, how badly he had "blown it." He had had it all — and lost it.

UNDERSTANDING TWO QUESTIONS

"Who Am I?"

Against this backdrop, after forty years, God spoke to Moses from the midst of a "burning" bush in the desert. "Therefore, come now, and I will send you to Pharaoh, so that you may bring My people, the sons of Israel, out of Egypt."[11] Forty years earlier Moses might have thought, "God, I don't know you very well, but I have to hand it to you, you certainly know how to pick 'em. If anyone can do a job like that, I surely can." But at eighty years of age, after forty years in the wilderness, Moses responds, "Who am I, that I should go to Pharaoh, and that I should bring the sons of Israel out of Egypt?" This is a changed Moses, a man with humility. Besides, forty years earlier he already tried what God was asking and it hadn't worked. Why should it be any different now? Moses had not yet understood the significance of his own pivotal question, "Who Am I?"

God's response to Moses is critical to my thesis: "Certainly I will be with you ..." The implication is obvious. When Moses tried to save his people forty years earlier he had done it on his own, presumably because he thought he was quite adequate alone. That's why he failed. This time it wouldn't be the adequacy of Moses but the power of God working through him that would guarantee success. At forty, Moses was the most educated and capable Jew in the world, a man of pride, the "pro." At eighty, he was a humbled man recognizing his need for God in order to truly succeed in his life and activities.

"Who am I?" or better, "Who do I think I am?" was the first critical question I faced as my own spiritual bottom line. Reluctance to admit my moral failure and need was a greater deterrent to confessing faith in Jesus as Lord than any other single factor.

"God, Who Are You?"

Moses is still not sure. He has a painful memory that he has carried for forty years, that is, the rebuff of his own people: "Who made you a ruler and judge over us?" they had asked. Fearing a repeat of this challenge, Moses asks, "God, who are you?" That is, "What is Your name, so that I can tell them who sent me?" God's answer is awesome, "I Am Who I Am." Moses is to go as the instrument of God the "I Am," the One without beginning or end, the forever present tense, the Eternal One. Moses questions further: "What if they will not believe me...?"[12] God proceeded to turn Moses' shepherd's crook into a snake and back again, and his hand leprous like snow and healed again. God was not dependent on Moses' education and capabilities. He has all the power in the universe. God made it clear to Moses that He was capable and desirous of filling yielded and humble human vessels with His love and power, so long as praise and credit were properly directed to the source of all goodness, to God Himself.

These are the two timeless questions each of us must face in mind and experience in coming to faith in Jesus Christ. In spite of our abilities, we must recognize that something is still missing from our lives. The paradox of power and humility that is evident in Moses' later life must be attractive to us. Moses was eulogized for "all the signs and wonders which the Lord sent him to perform in the land of Egypt against Pharaoh ... and for all the mighty power and for all the great terror ... he performed." Yet Moses was described as "very humble, more than any man who was on the face of the earth."[13] It is unlikely that he learned humility in the palace in Egypt. Maybe we, too, should consider a visit to the desert to learn shepherding.

APPLYING THE SPIRITUAL PRINCIPLE

The two questions, "Who Am I?" and "God, Who Are You?" were not formalized in my thinking at the time I was struggling with my own faith commitment. But the concept was. I realized that who I thought I was determined to a great extent how big my God could be. I had come across this idea in my reading of C.S. Lewis.

In God you come up against something which is in every respect immeasurably superior to yourself. Unless you know God as that — and, therefore, know yourself as nothing in comparison — you do not know God at all. As long as you are proud you cannot know God.[14]

> "...One's relationship to God and to Jesus Christ is strictly a personal relationship... One cannot remain neutral about Him."
>
> Charles Colson, former White House aide

I was both hesitant and incapable of making myself smaller, so to speak. It was not until God revealed to me how big He is, that I finally saw myself small in comparison. It changed the course of my life.

Recounting My Assets

I was born and raised in a small farm community of southeast South Dakota. This setting was hardly the stuff from which arrogance is generated, though in jest we would express our pride that at least we were not from the neighboring state of Iowa!

There were many assets that I inherited from my parents, but two stand out as having had prime importance to me. In fact, they were so important to me that I allowed them to become liabilities. The first asset was that I had good athletic ability. In hindsight it is apparent to me that my world of comparison was not very large, but from where I stood, I was "pretty good." Conference, regional and state championships in various sports gave me a basis for thinking I was better than others. This was reinforced regularly by the press coverage I would get in our local newspaper, a weekly. Front-page news included the local high school gridiron or other sports highlights. The more ink I got, the more my ego grew. The coaches first noticed a problem when each week they had to issue me a larger football helmet!

The second asset that I turned into a personal liability was intellectual acumen. High marks came easily for me, and my peers viewed me as a "brain." The recognition and awards I received in the academic area, added to my athletic achievements, were a formula that fueled my self-identity and values. At that point God was unnecessary — I was doing fine without Him. I wasn't so much arrogant as I was self-sufficient and conceited.

It was during sophomore biology lab that I met a girl who saw life differently. Vernee, too, was very capable, but talked about a personal relationship that she had with Jesus. This was her focal point in life, determining self-acceptance and values. She also had humility. I found her attractive and we began to spend time together. Her influence set me on a spiritual search which was several years in the making. It was also some years later that we married, and I have loved her, biology and the Lord to whom she pointed me ever since! However, the years until then produced a spiritual bankruptcy which set me on a new course.

Temporal Prosperity

My attending college was assumed. Sorting out the scholarship offers and holding out for the best deal was a palace experience (a la Moses), making me feel that I was in the driver's seat of my destiny. College years produced more athletic exploits, academic achievements, and even social recognition, as I was named king of the Valentine ball on campus.

Intellectually I was most impressed with the logical and rational, yet personable, faculty I met in the natural sciences. They were not cowed from their scientific convictions about human evolution in the face of criticism from what I then viewed as less informed and narrow religious types. My choice of a degree in biology and secondary education contained a crusade element; that is, I would go out and rescue the next generation from religious narrow-mindedness to this more-enlightened, scientific understanding.

The height of my vanity as "the pro" came during my first year as a high school teacher of general science, biology and chemistry. I received a telephone call from the chairman of a graduate biology program at a state university. He persuaded me to visit the university to become acquainted. But as I explained to him, the years of college with three varsity sports and a demanding science curriculum had left me tired. I wasn't immediately looking forward to graduate education. Nevertheless, I completed the application process, primarily because after teaching three months of general science to junior high school students, it was apparent to me that there were worse things than going back to school!

It was shortly after the Christmas holiday that I was called to my principal's office to receive a long-distance call. The same graduate school department chairman was calling to congratulate me on my acceptance to his biology department, and to inform me that I had been chosen as the recipient of a full-ride, national scholarship that would pay all educational expenses plus a stipend sufficient to live on for a four- to five-year Ph.D. program. I should have collapsed to my knees in tears of gratitude—but I didn't. I am embarrassed and ashamed to recall my thoughts as I headed back to my science laboratory: "When you're good enough, this kind of thing happens to you!" I imagined that I had earned that award. Instead of experiencing gratefulness, this was the ultimate ego-trip. I was going to be a Ph.D.!

Spiritual Bankruptcy

God must have had a good laugh, so to speak, over my pretension to have the world by the tail. Shortly after arriving at the university to begin graduate studies, I met some men — Christians — who did not fit my anti-intellectual stereotype. Some were even university Ph.D. scientists. None of them were pushy about their faith, but did defend it with evidences that I never knew existed. Particularly, I wondered how anyone could justify belief in a Bible that propagated such pre-science myths as special creation in six twenty-four-hour days, an actual hell (fire and all), and a real devil — to name a few. I knew better than that!

I don't recall any adversarial relationships with these men, but in my own heart I set out to prove that I was right. I began to read books they gave me on external evidences such as archaeology and manuscript studies. What a surprise to me that the New Testament writings were the most reliable of antiquity. Another man challenged me to read and critically study the New Testament writings firsthand. It was true that I had been acquainted with the Bible since I was a child, but I had not examined its truthfulness as an adult.

For the first time in my life I was applying the tools of evidence and reason to the investigation of faith. This educational process continued for months. I was spending as much time scrutinizing the Bible and books on evidence as I was on my graduate studies in biology. Little by little it dawned on me that I was wrong about almost everything on which my skepticism was based. The evidence about Christianity that I was learning had begun to satisfy my mind. But God was not close. I sensed no relationship there.

The interesting thing was that my reading kept bringing me back to focus on the person of Jesus. I was intrigued by Him — both attracted and repelled at the same time. I liked His life — compassionate, witty, sensitive, powerful, ethical, etc. But some of His teachings were threatening — absolute authority, uncompromising holiness, and unlimited forgiveness, even toward enemies. Secretly, like Peter the fishing "pro," I still thought these were some of the things that I knew better than Jesus.

My turning point came late one night in a most unexpected way. My wife Vernee had already gone to bed, leaving me alone to hit the books, as was my custom, into the wee hours of the morning. At some point I decided to read in the Bible for awhile. I don't recall why, but I was attracted to the Old Testament book of Job. Being competitive, I read with interest the challenge the devil presented to God concerning Job's life.[15] Reading the disaster that came to Job, I felt that God was unfair and I agreed with Job when he cried out that "God has wronged me."[16] I felt he was perfectly justified to say, "Nevertheles I will argue my ways before Him... Behold now, I have prepared my case ... let me speak, then reply to me."[17] I believed that God had some accounting to do. Who did He think He was anyway?

Job got his chance. I was as surprised as Job when God appeared and spoke to him: "Who is this that darkens My counsel with words without knowledge? Brace yourself like a man; I will question you, and you shall answer Me."[18] God spoke with tongue in cheek when He said He would sit at Job's feet so that He could learn from him! It's not possible to feel the full impact of this encounter without reading it in its entirety in Job 38-42. Some excerpts of God's questioning will serve only to give the sense of it:

Where were you when I laid the earth's foundation? Tell Me if you understand. Who marked off its dimensions? Surely you know!...

Have you ever given orders to the morning, or shown the dawn its place...

Have the gates of death been shown to you?...

Can you bind the beautiful Pleiades? Can you loose the cords of Orion? Can you bring forth the constellations in their seasons...?

Who endowed the heart with wisdom or gave understanding to the mind?...

These were all questions about the precision and splendor of the universe. It occurred to me that God must truly be "into science." This is where I was good. But these questions probed deeper into the mysteries of origins and functions than those in any exam I had ever taken. However, the best was yet to come — biology, my specialty.

Who provides food for the raven when its young cry out to God and wander about for lack of food?...

Who let the wild donkey go free? Who untied his ropes?...

Do you give the horse her strength or clothe his neck with a flowing mane?...

Does the hawk take flight by your wisdom and spread his wings toward the south? Does the eagle soar at your command and build his nest on high?

After two full chapters of scientific questions, God turned to Job: "Will the one who contends with the Almighty correct Him? Let him who accuses God answer Him!" Job's response was not what I expected: "I am unworthy — how can I reply to You? I put my hand over my mouth. I spoke once, but I have no answer—twice, but I will say no more."[19]

In my conceit, I thought Job's response was rather wimpy. Didn't he know anything about these matters? I did not yet see God as clearly as Job did.

God continued: "Would you discredit My justice? Would you condemn Me to justify yourself? Do you have an arm like God's, and can your voice thunder like His? ...Unleash the fury of your wrath, look at every proud man and bring him low ... Then I myself will admit to you that your own right hand can save you." What follows are two more chapters of questions concerning the order and design evident in the world.

Suddenly, in a profoundly personal way, God was no longer talking to Job — He was talking to me! Powerfully, though not audibly, I experienced the voice of God questioning, "Don, who do you think you are anyway?" My mind's eye flashed back to the many incidents of pride, envy, self-sufficiency, independence and conceit. God was revealing to me the true nature of my heart. In contrast to that, it seemed I was in the presence of a powerful, wise and righteous God. Job's final remarks described what I was experiencing:

I know that You can do all things; no plan of Yours can be thwarted.

You asked, "Who is this that obscures My counsel without knowledge?" Surely I spoke of things I did not understand, things too wonderful for me to know.

You said, "Listen now, and I will speak; I will question you, and you shall answer Me." My ears had heard of You but now my eyes have seen You. Therefore I despise myself and repent in dust and ashes.[20]

I slipped out of my chair to my knees and began to cry. A deep emotional thought possessed me: "Lord, I'm sorry!" Growing up, I had been conditioned to believe that strong people don't cry; that it was a sign of weakness in a man. But that night machismo didn't matter. I was devastated by the conviction of my sinfulness, and I could only repeat again and again, "I'm sorry—Lord, I'm sorry." I am not certain how much time had lapsed before I was surprised by an unexpected development.

I was still on my knees reflecting on the awesomeness of God and my new desire to be under His authority. It began with the thought that I was free — of my need to win, to be number one and to prove myself; of the slavery to my ego. I didn't have to perform any more. Oh, what a release! It was only then that I was flooded with the realization that I was forgiven. God's love through the sacrifice of Jesus, the Lamb of God, had paid it all. It was as if all the rules and regulations that I had associated with church and God were gone. Figuratively, in their place was a caring, personal God with outstretched arms saying, "Don, I love you." I humbly had to admit my spiritual bankruptcy and accept forgiveness as His gift to me. Tears were flowing again, this time not of regret. They were tears of joy as my heart cried, "Thank you ... Lord, thank you ... thank you!" I was a new man — forgiven and free.

Under New Management

Many years have passed since that eventful night. I went on to complete that Ph.D. in biology, and later an M.A. in New Testament studies, but not for my ego. The reality of a personal relationship with Jesus, whom I now knew to be very much alive, instilled in me accountability to my Creator and ultimate Judge. It is not as harsh as that may sound — it is the right combination of love and discipline. I have been set free to serve, and to become more myself under His Lordship than ever before — the way I was created to be. I am at peace — under new management.

What difference has Jesus made in my life? Let me be specific.

1. **I have received and continue to experience the forgiveness of my sin.**

"He died once for the sins of all us guilty sinners, although He Himself was innocent of any sin at any time, that He might bring us safely home to God."[21]

"If we confess our sins, He is faithful and just and will forgive us our sins and purify us from all unrighteousness."[22]

2. **I am a spiritual child of God and enabled to follow Him by the Holy Spirit within me.**

"Yet to all who received Him, to those who believed in His name, He gave the right to become children of God..."[23]

"But the Counselor, the Holy Spirit, whom the Father will send in My name, will teach you all things and will remind you of everything I have said to you."[24]

3. **I am at peace with God and do not fear judgment.**

"For God did not send the Son into the world to judge the world; but that the world should be saved through Him. He who believes in Him is not judged..."[25]

"There is therefore now no condemnation for those who are in Christ Jesus. For the law of the Spirit of life in Christ Jesus has set you free from the law of sin and of death."[26]

4. **I have the assurance of eternal life after death.**

"I am the resurrection and the life; he who believes in Me will live even if he dies..."[27]

"These things I have written to you who believe in the name of the Son of God, in order that you may know that you have eternal life."[28]

It must be understood that I do not claim these because I consider myself worthy, or have done some deed to earn them. The Bible says, "Because of His kindness you have been saved through trusting Christ. And even trusting is not of yourselves; it too is a gift from God. Salvation is not a reward for the good we have done, so none of us can take any credit for it."[29] My wife, Vernee, and I both recognize that we would not have stayed together in marriage for more than forty years now if not for the grace to forgive and change — which comes from Him. Our two sons have come to acknowledge Jesus as Savior and Lord. What hope there is in knowing that when our family relationship here must end, death will only serve to reunite us once again, this time for all eternity. Every aspect of my life has been enriched under the new management of Jesus Christ.

> "Following Jesus Christ has been an experience of increasing challenge, adventure and happiness. He is totally worthwhile. How true are His words: 'I am come that they might have life, and that they might have it more abundantly.'"
> Mark Hatfield, former U.S. Senator from Oregon

A PERSONAL INVITATION

Clark Pinnock has expressed in a succinct way what I have personally discovered about faith in my life journey.

I am convinced that faith needs to face up to the truth question and that the Christian message fits the facts. It is not a presupposition that has to be accepted on authority or a self-evident truth that needs no argument; it is a solid truth claim that can be tested and verified across the whole range of human experience. It meets our existential needs, makes sense out of our religious intuitions, stands up under rational scrutiny, corresponds with the historical evidence and speaks to today's moral necessities...

To stand beneath the lordship of Christ is not a misfortune or humiliation for you. It is rather the entrance into abundant life and an existence that is truly desirable.

Therefore, I make this appeal to you: open yourself up to God, confess your failure to live a just and holy life, and determine to follow the Lord Jesus. Act upon the evidence that stands before you and accept the saving offer that is being extended.[30]

The Bible says that Jesus came "to seek and to save that which was lost."[31] Jesus respects your will. He waits for an invitation — a commitment on your part to ask Him to forgive you and take the wheel. No one can say it better than He did.

Come to Me, all you who are weary and burdened, and I will give you rest. Take My yoke upon you and learn from Me, for I am gentle and humble in heart, and you will find rest for your souls. For My yoke is easy and My burden is light.[32]

The apostle Paul promised that "if you confess with your mouth Jesus as Lord, and believe in your heart that God raised Him from the dead, you shall be saved..."[33]

These promises don't mean much until you reach out and take them for yourself. If you are ready to move into a relationship with God through faith in Jesus Christ, tell Him so through prayer. This simple prayer may be used if you are not sure what to say:

Dear God, thank your for providing us evidence for Your existence. I want to know the reality of a personal relationship with You. I acknowledge that my sin has separated me from You. I repent, and confess Jesus Christ as my Savior and Lord. I believe He died in my place and that you raised Him from the dead. Please give me the gift of the Holy Spirit to direct my life, and enable me to understand and follow Your Word from this day on. Thank You for making me Your spiritual child and giving me the assurance of eternal life. Amen.

— FOCUS & DISCUSSION —

1. It is stated in the text that a refusal to admit one's own identity as a sinner is a greater deterrent to recognizing Jesus' deity than any other single factor. Explain. Can you relate to this personally?

2. What two questions must each person ask and honestly answer along the path to faith? How are they related?

3. What is the "bottom line" in a person's getting right with God? Why is pride or self-sufficiency such a difficult thing to deal with? Is the difficulty primarily intellectual in nature?

4. What if someone said, "Becoming a Christian is the easiest thing in the world." What do you think they mean by that?

5. What does the fact that salvation is a gift imply about a Christian's basis for assurance of eternal life? What is it dependent upon?

Taking The Next Step

Congratulations on completing your reading of *Surprised by Faith*. I hope it was helpful in your pursuit of knowing God, answering your questions about faith, or that it strengthened and deepened your existing faith. Whatever happened in your life as a result of *Surprised by Faith*, I would like to hear about it. Use one of the communication means below or complete the card inside the back cover of this book—it would be encouraging to me.

I made a faith-commitment to follow Jesus. Now what?

Your commitment to follow Jesus Christ is the most significant one you will ever make. Therefore, I invite you to take the next step that will assure your future spiritual fulfillment. The Bible says,

"And now just as you trusted Christ to save you, trust Him, too, for each day's problems.... See that you go on growing in the Lord, and become strong and vigorous..." (Colossians 2:6-7, TLB).

Jesus made a promise to us when He said, "I came that they might have life, and might have it abundantly" (John 10:10). The difference between a "so-so" faith and the abundant life Jesus promised is found in building our relationship with God through the study of His Word, the Bible. I have written another book that will guide you in that meaningful and exciting process.

If you made a faith commitment to trust and follow Jesus Christ for the first time as a result of reading *Surprised by Faith*, I want to provide you with a <u>free copy</u> of my book, *Growing Faith*. Use the card at the back of this book or one of the communication means identified below and provide your name, mailing address, telephone, e-mail, and indicate your age as Jr. High or Sr. High, 19-54 or 55+.

For a free copy of *Growing Faith*, to request further help, or to express comments:

Dr. Don Bierle, *FaithSearch*, 105 Peavey Road, Suite 200, Chaska, MN 55318, U.S.A.
E-mail: sbf@faithsearch.org • Telephone: 952-401-4501

What if I have more questions or suggestions?

On the other hand, you may have read this book and still have questions. Indeed, you may have objections or an evaluation concerning the contents. In any case, I invite your questions or comments. The subject of Jesus Christ is important enough to justify taking another step to resolve whatever questions or objections that may remain. Use the card at the back of the book or one of the communication means above that is most convenient for you. I look forward to hearing from you.

Discovering the *Ah-ha!* of Life

EVENTS AND RESOURCES
Watch for these EVENTS by Dr. Don Bierle

Dr. Don Bierle travels nationally and internationally to present the following events. Contact his office using the address below, for further information and scheduling.

FaithSearch Discovery: Discovering the "Ah-ha!" of Life

FaithSearch **Discovery** presents an inspiringly, breathtakingly logical case for believing in the historical person of Jesus Christ. Based on Dr. Bierle's book *Surprised by Faith*, this dynamic, live presentation is for everyone who wonders why they should believe, and for everyone who wonders why they do. *FaithSearch* **Discovery** has challenged, inspired and wonderfully changed hundreds of thousands of people, providing satisfying answers to life's important questions.

- Why am I here?
- Is Jesus really God?
- How can I know God?
- Is the Bible true?
- Can faith be reasonable?

FaithSearch Origins: *Making Sense of Creation & Evolution*

Biologist Donald A. Bierle, Ph.D., uses current scientific evidence to unravel creation, evolution and the meaning of life. His emphasis on the powerful concept of intelligent design will unite rather than divide people on this controversial subject. Stimulating and challenging, *FaithSearch* **Origins** is ideal for students, teachers, pastors and parents.

FaithSearch Destiny: Making Sense of Life after Death

Using logic, and biblical and historical evidence, *FaithSearch* **Destiny** separates truth from fiction concerning the afterlife. This compelling presentation covers critical issues about the existence of God, the claims of reincarnation, the historical evidence for the resurrection of Jesus, fulfilled prophecy and the end of the world. *Making Sense of Life after Death* provides answers to questions each person should resolve about the course of life... and death.

To learn more about Dr. Bierle's events and resources, call or write:

FaithSearch International
105 Peavey Road, STE 200, Chaska, MN 55318, USA
Ph: 952-401-4501 or 1-800-964-1447
E-mail: info@faithsearch.org
Or visit our Web site at **www.faithsearch.org**

The FaithSearch Participant Guide

The *FaithSearch Participant Guide* is the perfect companion to *FaithSearch Discovery*. It covers the complete content of the presentation, including thought-provoking questions (and answers), supporting material and suggestions for further study. More than just a seminar workbook, the *Guide* also offers brief, insightful articles addressing questions asked most-frequently at a *FaithSearch*.

FaithSearch: Youth

This workbook presents *FaithSearch* with the younger person in mind. It is *Surprised by Faith* in interactive, question-and-answer form. This unique study tool conducts a virtual field trip through the New Testament to discover what eyewitnesses to Jesus actually saw and heard.

FaithSearch Origins:
Making Sense of Creation and Evolution Seminar Notes

Scientist and former skeptic Don Bierle has authored a valuable resource that captures the content of his popular *FaithSearch* **Origins** event. *Making Sense of Creation and Evolution* is more than just a companion piece to the presentation, however. The text is full of insight and current scientific information, and includes useful references to books and Internet sites for further reading and research.

FaithSearch Destiny:
Making Sense of Life after Death

Designed to help people get the most from the *FaithSearch* **Destiny** event, Dr. Bierle has authored *Making Sense of Life after Death*. Easy to follow, this publication also includes a wealth of Scripture references for personal study. Like the presentation, it explains and outlines the way to a personal relationship with God and the basis for assurance of eternal life after death.

FaithSearch Discipleship:
Growing Faith

This discipleship manual contains eight easy-to-follow lessons that help a person get firmly rooted in the truth of God's Word, the Bible. Each lesson is intellectually and spiritually challenging, leading the user through selected readings and key Scripture passages that help them understand what God has done and will do in their life. *Growing Faith* includes daily Bible readings and focus questions, as well as resources to expand and deepen your understanding of the Christian faith, on topics such as the Holy Spirit, overcoming doubt and temptation, learning to pray, and the importance of fellowship in the church. (*Leader's Guide* also available.)

FaithSearch Influence:
Friend to Friend

Friend to Friend is a positive outreach and discipleship strategy that removes the "cookie-cutter" nature of some approaches. It empowers every Christian to become involved through relationships in his or her networks of influence. The event presents the foundational principles for successful outreach and discipleship for the entire church, using **FaithSearch** events and resources. (Available as: *Friend to Friend* Student Manual and Leader's Guide.)

BIBLIOGRAPHY

This bibliography is only a selection of resources that the interested reader can turn to for additional information about topics addressed in this book. Those seeking more details about specific references in the text should consult the footnotes identified throughout the chapters. They list the sources used and also give page numbers.

BOOKS

Archer, Gleason L. *Encyclopedia of Bible Difficulties*. Grand Rapids: Zondervan, 1982.

Barnett, Paul. *Is the New Testament Reliable?* Downers Grove, Ill.: InterVarsity Press, 1986.

Blaiklock, E.M. and R.K. Harrison, eds. *The New International Dictionary of Biblical Archaeology*. Grand Rapids: Zondervan, 1983.

Blomberg, Craig. *The Historical Reliability of the Gospels*. Downers Grove, Ill.: InterVarsity Press, 1987.

Bowman, Robert, Jr. *Why You Should Believe in the Trinity*. Grand Rapids: Baker, 1989.

Boyd, Gregory and Edward Boyd. *Letters From A Skeptic*. Wheaton, Ill.: Victor, 1994.

Bruce, F.F. *Jesus and Christian Origins Outside the New Testament*. Grand Rapids: Eerdmans, 1974.

Bruce, F.F. *The Canon of Scripture*. Downers Grove, Ill.: InterVarsity Press, 1988.

Bruce, F.F. *The New Testament Documents: Are They Reliable?* Downers Grove, Ill.: InterVarsity Press, 1990.

Comfort, Philip W. ed. *The Origin of the Bible*. Wheaton, Ill.: Tyndale House, 1992.

Craig, William Lane. *Knowing the Truth about the Resurrection*. Ann Arbor, Mich.: Servant Books, 1988.

Craig, William Lane. *The Son Rises: Historical Evidence for the Resurrection of Jesus*. Chicago: Moody Press, 1981.

Geisler, Norman and Ron Brooks. *When Skeptics Ask: A Handbook on Christian Evidences*. Wheaton, Ill.: Victor, 1990.

Geisler, Norman and Thomas Howe, *When Critics Ask: A Popular Handbook of Bible Difficulties*. Wheaton, Ill.: Victor, 1992.

Geisler, Norman and William Nix. *A General Introduction to the Bible*. Chicago: Moody Press, 1986.

Geivett, R. Douglas, and Gary Habermas, eds. *In Defense of Miracles*. Downers Grove, Ill.: InterVarsity Press, 1997.

Green, Michael. *Who Is This Jesus?* Nashville: Nelson, 1992.

Groothuis, Douglas. *Jesus in an Age of Controversy*. Eugene, Ore.: Harvest House, 1996.

Groothuis, Douglas. *Revealing the New Age Jesus*. Downers Grove, Ill.: InterVarsity Press, 1990.

Habermas, Gary. *Ancient Evidence for the Life of Jesus*. Nashville: Nelson, 1984.

Habermas, Gary and Antony Flew. *Did Jesus Rise From the Dead? The Resurrection Debate*. San Francisco: Harper & Row, 1987.

Kaiser, Walter, Jr. *Hard Sayings of the Bible*. Downers Grove, Ill.: InterVarsity Press, 1997.

McDowell, Josh and Bill Wilson. *He Walked Among Us*. Nashville: Nelson, 1994.

McRay, John. *Archaeology and the New Testament*. Grand Rapids: Baker, 1991.

Nash, Ronald. *Is Jesus the Only Savior?* Grand Rapids: Zondervan, 1994.

Neill, Stephen. *Christian Faith & Other Faiths*. Downers Grove, Ill.: InterVarsity Press, 1984.

Price, Randall. *The Stones Cry Out*. Eugene, Ore.: Harvest House, 1997.

Sanders, John. *What About Those Who Have Never Heard?* Downers Grove, Ill.:InterVarsity Press, 1995.

Schaeffer, Francis. *Escape From Reason*. Downers Grove, Ill.: InterVarsity Press, 1968. Ch.7.

Schaeffer, Francis. *The God Who Is There*. Downers Grove, Ill.: InterVarsity Press, 1968. Sec.I, Chs.1,5; Sec.II, Chs.1,2,& 5; Sects.III,IV,& V.

Schaeffer, Francis. *He Is There and He Is Not Silent*. Wheaton, Ill.: Tyndale House, 1972.

Stevenson, Kenneth and Gary Habermas. *The Shroud and the Controversy*. Nashville: Nelson, 1990.

Strobel, Lee. *The Case for Christ*. Grand Rapids: Zondervan, 1998.

Strobel, Lee. *The Case for Faith*. Grand Rapids: Zondervan, 2000.

Wilkins, Michael J., and J.P. Moreland, eds. *Jesus under Fire*. Grand Rapids: Zondervan, 1995.

ARTICLES

Fine, Steven. "Why Bone Boxes?" *Biblical Archaeology Review* 27 (Sept./Oct. 2001).

Greenhut, Zvi. "Burial Cave of the Caiaphas Family", *Biblical Archaeology Review* 18 (Sept/Oct, 1992).

Lemaire, Andre. "Burial Box of James the Brother of Jesus", *Biblical Archaeology Review* V. 28 No. 6 (Nov/Dec, 2002).

Lemonick, Michael D. "Are the Bible's Stories True?", *Time* 146 (December 18, 1995):62-70.

Shanks, Hershel ed., "New Analysis of the Crucified Man", *Biblical Archaeology Review* 11 (Nov/Dec, 1985).

Tzaferis, Vassilios "Crucifixion—The Archaeological Evidence," *Biblical Archaeology Review* 9 (Jan/Feb 1985).

JOURNALS

Biblical Archaeology Review. P.O. Box 7026; Red Oak, IA 51591. Published quarterly.

Biblical Illustrator. Customer Service, One LifeWay Plaza, Nashville, TN 37234. Published quarterly.

Christian Research Journal. P.O. Box 500; San Juan Capistrano, CA 92693. Published quarterly.

Notes

Chapter One: Why Am I Here?

1. Clark Pinnock, *A Case for Faith* (Minneapolis: Bethany, 1980), p. 24.

2. John Lennon & Paul McCartney, "Nowhere Man" (Northern Songs Ltd., 1965), recorded on *Rubber Soul.*

3. Michael Cassidy, *Christianity for the Open-Minded* (Downers Grove, IL: InterVarsity Press, 1978), p. 12.

4. An ecologist would suggest that grass finds meaning in returning to the soil in a natural cycle of nutrients. But this requires death, the sacrifice of the individual, for some undemonstrated higher cause. We are concerned here with where natural laws came from and what meaning they have beyond finite existence.

5. Pinnock, p. 34.

6. Paul Little, *Know Why You Believe* (Downers Grove, IL: InterVarsity, 1988), p. 15.

7. Francis A. Schaeffer, *The Complete Works of Francis A. Schaeffer: A Christian Worldview,* vol. 1: A Christian View of Philosophy and Culture (Westchester, IL: Crossway Books, 1982), pp. 101ff.

8. Michael D. Lemonick, "Are the Bible's Stories True?", *Time* 146 (December 18, 1995):62-70.

Chapter Two: Is The Bible True?

1. For this evidence, see F.F. Bruce, *Jesus and Christian Origins Outside the New Testament* (Grand Rapids, MI: Eerdmans, 1974); and Gary R. Habermas, *Ancient Evidence for the Life of Jesus* (Nashville: Thomas Nelson, 1984).

2. Lee Strobel, *The Case for Christ* (Grand Rapids, MI: Zondervan, 1998), p. 81.

3. Taken from her regular column in the *Star and Tribune* newspaper of Minneapolis/St. Paul. Date unknown.

4. Julius Caesar, *The Gallic Wars*, (Norwalk, CT: Easton Press, 1983).

5. See the following sources for information on the numbers of various manuscripts: Bruce Metzger, *Chapters in the History of New Testament Textual Criticism* (Grand Rapids, MI: Eerdmans, 1963), pp. 144-151; F.F. Bruce, *The New Testament Documents: Are They Reliable?* (Grand Rapids, MI: Eerdmans, 1990), pp. 14-15; and Norman Geisler and William Nix, *A General Introduction to the Bible* (Chicago: Moody Press, 1986), pp. 385-408.

6. Bruce Metzger, as quoted in Strobel, p.63.

7. F.F. Bruce, *The Books and the Parchments* (Westwood, N.J.: Fleming H. Revell, 1963), p. 178.

8. Frederic Kenyon, *Our Bible and the Ancient Manuscripts* (New York: Harper & Brothers, 1941), p. 23.

9. Harold J. Greenlee, *Introduction to New Testament Textual Criticism*, rev. ed. (Peabody, MA: Hendrickson Publishers, 1999), p. 6.

10. Josh McDowell, editor, *Evidence that Demands a Verdict*, rev. ed. (San Bernardino, CA: Here's Life Publishers, 1979), pp. 41-42.

11. Philip Comfort, "Texts and Manuscripts of the New Testament" in *The Origin of the Bible*, Philip Comfort, ed. (Wheaton, IL: Tyndale House Publishers, 1992), pp. 179, 193.

12. Paul Barnett, *Is the New Testament Reliable? A Look at the Historical Evidence* (Downers Grove, IL: InterVarsity Press, 1986), p. 39.

13. David Van Biema, "The Gospel Truth?" *Time* 147 (April 8, 1996): 52-60.

14. Comfort, p. 180.

15. Frederic Kenyon, *The Bible and Modern Scholarship* (London: John Murray, 1948), p. 20.

16. Bruce, *The New Testament Documents: Are They Reliable?*, p. 15.

17. Metzger, *Chapters in the History of New Testament Textual Criticism*, pp. 144-151.

18. Geisler and Nix, p. 475.

19. Bruce, *The New Testament Documents: Are They Reliable?*, pp. 19-20.

20. Geisler and Nix, p. 431.

21. Bruce Metzger, *The Text of the New Testament: Its Transmission, Corruption, and Restoration*, (New York: Oxford University Press, 1992), p. 86.

22. Kenyon, *Our Bible and the Ancient Manuscripts*, p. 23.

23. Frederic Kenyon, *The Bible and Archaeology* (New York: Harper & Brothers, 1940), pp. 288f.

24. Luke 3:1-2a (NIV)

25. Bruce, *The New Testament Documents: Are They Reliable?*, p. 82.

26. David Van Biema, "The Brother of Jesus?", *Time* 160, (November 4, 2002):70.

27. Andre Lemaire, "Burial Box of James the Brother of Jesus", *Biblical Archaeology Review* 28 (Nov/Dec, 2002):24-33.

28. Matthew 13:55

29. Galatians 2:9; Acts 21:18

30. Hershel Shanks, "Cracks in James Bone Box Repaired," *Biblical Archaeology Review* 29 (Jan/Feb, 2003):20-25.

31. Joe Nickell, "Bone (Box) of Contention: The James Ossuary," *Skeptical Inquirer* (March/April, 2003):19-22.

32. See Flavius Josephus, *Antiquities of the Jews* (Grand Rapids, MI: AP&A), book XVIII, ch. 3, paragraph 3, p. 379; and Bruce, *Jesus and Christian Origins Outside the New Testament*, p. 22.

33. Robert Bull, "Caesarea Maritima — The Search for Herod's City," *Biblical Archaeology Review* 8 (May/June, 1982):24-41.

34. Luke 3:1-2

35. Zvi Greenhut, "Burial Cave of the Caiaphas Family," *Biblical Archaeology Review* 18 (Sept/Oct, 1992):28-36.

36. C.A. Evans, "Caiaphas Ossuary,"in S.E. Porter and C.A. Evans, *Dictionary of New Testament Background. A compendium of contemporary biblical scholarship*, electronic ed. (Downers Grove, IL: InterVarsity, 2000).

37. Luke 2:1-2 (NIV)

38. Randall Price, *The Stones Cry Out: What Archaeology Reveals About the Bible* (Eugene, OR: Harvest House, 1997), p. 299.

39. Luke 3:23

40. Price, p. 299.

41. See both Paul L. Maier, *First Christmas* (San Francisco: Harper & Row, 1971), pp. 15-22; and Habermas, *Ancient Evidence for the Life of Jesus*, pp. 152-53.

42. J.R. McRay, "Archaeology and the New Testament: 4. Jesus and His World," and B. Chilton and E. Yamauchi, "Synagogues: 4. Remains of Buildings," in Porter and Evans.

43. Luke 7:1-5

44. McRay, "Archaeology and the New Testament: 4. Jesus and His World," in Porter and Evans.

45. Luke 2:22

46. John 5:1-5

47. John 9:1-12

48. Luke 8:26-33. See also McRay, "Archaeology and the New Testament: 4. Jesus and His World," in Porter and Evans.

49. Vassilios Tzaferis, "Crucifixion—The Archaeological Evidence," *Biblical Archaeology Review* 9 (Jan/Feb 1985):44-53.

50. Hershel Shanks, ed., "New Analysis of the Crucified Man," *Biblical Archaeology Review* 11 (Nov/Dec, 1985):20-21.

51. Tzaferis, p. 52.

52. John 19:32-33 (NIV)

53. Tzaferis, p. 53. Zias and Sekeles later published their opinion that in the case of this crucifixion victim, the leg bones may have been broken postmortem, rather than as a final *coup de grâce*. See "The Crucified Man from Giv'at ha-Mivtar: A Reappraisal," *Israel Exploration Journal*, Vol. 35, No. 1 (1985), pp. 22-27.

54. Acts 17:6. Politarchs is a transliteration from the original Greek and is usually translated to English as "city authorities" or "rulers" in our New Testaments.

55. McRay, "Archaeology and the New Testament: 5. The World of the Early Church," in Porter and Evans.

56. Bruce, *The New Testament Documents: Are They Reliable?*, p. 82.

57. William M Ramsay, *The Bearing of Recent Discovery on the Trustworthiness of the New Testament* (Grand Rapids, MI: Baker Book House, 1979 reprint), pp. 81, 222.

58. W.F. Albright, *The Archaeology of Palestine*, rev. ed. (Baltimore: Pelican Books, 1960), pp. 127f.

59. Millar Burrows, *What Mean These Stones?* (New York: Meridian Books, 1956), p. 1.

60. Nelson Glueck, *Rivers in the Desert: A history of the Negev* (Philadelphia: Jewish Publications Society of America, 1969), p. 31.

61. Kenyon, *The Bible and Archaeology*, p. 279.

62. K.A. Kitchen, *The Bible in its World* (Downers Grove, IL: InterVarsity Press, 1977), p. 132.

63. Acts 2:22-23, 32-33

64. Acts 2:41

65. Acts 26:26

66. Bruce, *The New Testament Documents: Are They Reliable?*, p. 46.

67. Julius Muller's critique of D.F. Strauss' theory that the Gospel accounts are mere legends has never been answered: "Most decidedly must a considerable interval of time be required for such

a complete transformation of a whole history by popular tradition, when the series of legends are formed in the same territory where the heroes actually lived and wrought. Here one cannot imagine how such a series of legends could arise in an historical age, obtain universal respect, and supplant the historical recollection of the true character and connecting of their heroes' lives in the minds of the community, if eyewitnesses were still at hand, who could be questioned respecting the truth of the recorded marvels. Hence, legendary fiction, as it likes not the clear present time, but prefers the mysterious gloom of grey antiquity, is wont to seek a remoteness of age, along with that of space, and to remove its boldest and more rare and wonderful creations into a very remote and unknown land." Julius Muller, *The Theory of Myths, in its Application to the Gospel History, Examined and Confuted* (London: John Chapman, 1844), p. 26; in William Craig, *The Son Rises* (Chicago: Moody Press, 1981), p. 101.

68. A.N. Sherwin-White, *Roman Society and Roman Law in the New Testament*, (Oxford: Clarendon Press, 1963), p. 190.

69. A.N. Sherwin-White, cited in Pinnock, p. 77.

70. Bruce, *The New Testament Documents: Are They Reliable?*, p. 88.

71. Sidney Collett, *All About the Bible* (New York: Revell, 1934), pp. 62-63.

72. Sherwin-White, p. 189.

73. William Ramsay as cited in Norman Geisler and Thomas Howe, *When Critics Ask. A Popular Handbook on Bible Difficulties* (Wheaton, IL: Victor Books, 1992), p. 385.

74. C.S. Lewis, *Surprised by Joy* (London: Collins, 1955), pp. 178f, 182, 187f.

75. Frank Morison, *Who Moved the Stone?* (Grand Rapids: Zondervan, 1977 reprint), pp. 8-12.

Chapter Three: Is Jesus Really God?

1. Luke 2:52

2. See Luke 4:14-30.

3. Isaiah 61:1-2

4. It may be argued that Jesus' claim to be the Messiah would not necessarily be a claim of divinity. But in view of His challenge in Matthew 22:41-46, He undoubtedly intended it as a claim to be God as well. In Luke 4:18-19, Jesus quoted from Isaiah 61:1-2. According to the same Old Testament book (9:6), the Messiah was called, "Mighty God, Eternal Father." Jesus' certain familiarity with this latter passage would mean that His claim to be the Messiah was also a claim to be God.

5. John 4:25-26; Mark 8:27-30

6. See Matthew 22:41-46.

7. R.V.G. Tasker, *The Gospel According to St. Matthew* (Grand Rapids, MI: Eerdmans, 1978), p. 213. In the *Tyndale New Testament Commentaries*.

8. See John 8:53-59.

9. See Exodus 3:14.

10. See John 10:22-33.

11. See John 8:23-24.

12. See John 5:21; 10:27-28; 11:25-26.

13. See Matthew 28:18.

14. John 19:7

15. John W. Montgomery, *History and Christianity* (Minneapolis: Bethany, 1965), p. 63.

16. See Luke 5:17-26.

17. Luke 5:24-26

18. John 9:1-3

19. Based on Jesus' response to two tragedies of His day recorded in Luke 13:1-5, i.e., the murder of some Galileans by Pilate and the

accidental death of 18 people when a tower fell on them, it is clear that He did not teach that all consequences that occur in life are the result of our personal sin. He did say, however, that sin is so serious that it results in death. Since we have all sinned, He said that we are in need of repentance in order to be saved from death.

20. Luke 7:11-16

21. See Luke 8:22-25.

22. Matthew 7:28-29. See also John 4:14; 8:12; and 11:25 for examples.

23. John 10:37-38 (NIV)

24. See Luke 4:1-13; Matthew 14:33; 28:17; and John 9:38.

25. Compare Matthew 4:10 with Deuteronomy 6:13.

26. Compare Matthew 21:15-16 with Psalm 8:2.

27. See Luke 4:33-36 and Matthew 12:24.

28. John 8:46 (NIV)

29. John 14:6

30. See Mark 10:45 with Psalm 49:7-9.

31. Luke 9:20 (NIV)

32. Jon A. Buell and O. Quentin Hyder, *Jesus: God, Ghost or Guru?* (Grand Rapids, MI: Zondervan, 1978), p. 102.

33. For example, see Matthew 16:21; 17:9; 26:32.

34. John 2:19

35. Michael Green, *Man Alive* (Downers Grove, IL: InterVarsity Press, 1968), pp. 53-54, as quoted in McDowell, p. 193-194.

36. Luke 24:11

37. John 19:39-40 (NIV)

38. John 20:4-8

39. John 20:24-29

40. Matthew 28:11-15

41. Paul L. Maier, *First Easter* (San Francisco: Harper and Row, 1973), p.120.

42. 1 Corinthians 15:5-6

43. C.H. Dodd, "The Appearances of the Risen Christ: A study in the form criticism of the Gospels," in *More New Testament Studies* (Manchester: U. of Manchester Press, 1968), p. 128.

44. Luke 24:39

45. Luke 24:41-43

46. See John 7:5, 1 Corinthians 15:7 and Acts 15:13.

47. For the apostle Paul's own testimony see Acts 9:1-22.

48. See Matthew 26:56, 69-75; John 20:19.

49. Gary Habermas, *The Resurrection of Jesus* (New York: University Press of America, 1984), p. 39.

50. J.N.D. Anderson, *The Evidence for the Resurrection* (Downers Grove, IL: InterVarsity Press, 1966), pp. 3-4.

51. C.S. Lewis, *Mere Christianity* (New York: Macmillan, 1952), pp. 55-56.

52. Edwin Yamauchi as quoted in Strobel, p. 90.

53. John 11:25-26

Chapter Four: Can Faith Be Reasonable?

1. Romans 10:13-17

2. J.B. Phillips, *The New Testament in Modern English* (New York: Macmillan, 1958), Romans 10:17.

3. See 1 Corinthians 15:12-19.

4. Acts 4:12

5. Romans 10:16-21 (NIV)

6. Matthew 21:28-32 (NIV)

7. James 2:17 (NIV)

8. Luke 6:46-49

9. See Genesis 15:1-6 and 22:1-19 for this discussion of Abraham.

10. Genesis 22:2

11. Hebrews 11:17-19 (NIV)

12. For evidence concerning this identification, see 2 Chronicles 3:1; 1 Chronicles 21:15-30; Book of Jubilees 18:13; Josephus (*Antiquities* I. xii. 1; VII. xiii. 4).

13. John 1:29

14. Galatians 3:6-9 (NIV)

15. See Romans 4:16-25 (NIV).

16. John 7:37-39 (NIV)

17. John 14:15-17, 23

18. 1 Corinthians 6:19 (NIV)

19. Ephesians 1:13-14 (NIV)

20. John 3:1-18

21. Bertrand Russell, *A History of Western Philosophy* (New York: Simon and Schuster, 1945).

22. Mark 7:20-23 (NIV)

23. G.K. Chesterton, *Orthodoxy* (Wheaton, IL: H. Shaw Publishers, 1994), pg. 11.

24. Ephesians 2:8-9 (NIV)

25. Romans 3:10-11

26. John 6:44

27. Titus 3:3-7 (NIV)

28. J. Gresham Machen, *The Christian Faith in the Modern World* (New York: The Macmillan Company, 1936).

29. Philippians 2:13 (NIV)

30. 1 John 5:11-13 (NIV)

31. John 3:16

32. Romans 6:23

33. McDowell, pp. 327-28.

34. John 14:1-3 (NIV)

35. See John 5:21-29 and 12:48.

36. Romans 8:1-2 (NIV)

Chapter Five: Where Am I?

1. Elizabeth Elliot, *Through Gates of Splendor* (New York: Harper, 1957).

2. Ephesians 4:18 (NIV)

3. 1 Timothy 1:13

4. For examples see Matthew 16:21; Mark 9:31; 10:32-34; John 2:19-22.

5. John 20:24-29 (NIV)

6. See Numbers 13 and 14.

7. Numbers 14:11 (NIV)

8. See Luke 7:2-10.

9. This discussion of Noah is based on the text in Genesis 6-8.

10. Hebrews 11:7

11. 1 Peter 3:18 (NIV)

12. Romans 10:9 (NIV)

13. John 1:12 (NIV)

14. C.S. Lewis, *The Screwtape Letters* (West Chicago: Lord and King Associates, 1976), p. 51.

15. See John 10:17-18; Mark 10:45; and Matthew 26:53.

16. See Matthew 26:47-56 and 27:38-54.

17. John 10:10 (NIV)

18. John 14:1-3

19. See 2 Peter 3:3-13 (NIV).

Chapter Six: How Can I Know God?

1. Quotes taken from *Sports Spectrum* Magazine, used by permission: Art Stricklin, "The Transformation," (March 2000): 17,19; and Paul Azinger, "Only God Changes Hearts," (March 2000):20,21.

2. Luke 5:1-11 (NIV)

3. A similar response using the same Greek word "kurios" is given by Thomas in John 20:28.

4. Luke 5:31-32 (NIV)

5. For background on John the Baptist, see Mark 1:1-8; 6:14-32; Luke 1:13-17; 3:1-20.

6. John 1:26-30

7. John 3:26-30

8. Luke 7:28 (NIV)

9. For the biblical accounts of Moses' life see Exodus 2 and 3, and Acts 7:17-38.

10. Acts 7:25

11. See Exodus 3:10-22 for this historical event.

12. See Exodus 4:1-17.

13. See Deuteronomy 34:10-12 and Numbers 12:3 for this paradox.

14. C.S. Lewis, *Mere Christianity*, p. 111.

15. See Job 1 and 2.

16. Job 19:6-7

17. Job 13:15-22

18. Job 38:2-3 (NIV)

19. Job 40:1-5 (NIV)

20. Job 42:2-6 (NIV)

21. 1 Peter 3:18 (TLB)

22. 1 John 1:9 (NIV)

23. John 1:12 (NIV)

24. John 14:26 (NIV)

25. John 3:17-18

26. Romans 8:1-2

27. John 11:25

28. 1 John 5:13

29. Ephesians 2:8-9 (TLB)

30. Pinnock, pp. 119, 121-2.

31. Luke 19:10

32. Matthew 11:28-30 (NIV)

33. Romans 10:9

TAKING THE NEXT STEP

Congratulations on completing your reading of *Surprised by Faith*. If it was helpful in your pursuit of God, answered some questions you had about faith, or strengthened your existing faith, please let me know. Simply check the appropriate box(es), adding your comments or questions below and return this card to me today. (Don't forget to affix appropriate postage.)

Ron

Dr. Don Bierle

❑ Yes, I've prayed for the first time to <u>begin</u> trusting Jesus as Savior and Lord of my life as a result of reading *Surprised by Faith*. Please send me a FREE copy of your book, *Growing Faith*, to help me start growing in relationship with God.

❑ I have prayed to <u>renew</u> my faith in Jesus as Savior and Lord of my life as a result of reading *Surprised by Faith*. Please send a FREE Bible study lesson from your book, *Growing Faith*, and tell me how I can get a complete copy to strengthen my faith.

❑ No, I am not ready to trust and follow Jesus as Savior and Lord of my life. Please have someone call or send information about the following questions or concerns.

Comments/Questions: _____

_____

_____

_____

❑ I'm interested in knowing more about getting involved with *FaithSearch*. Please call or send information about opportunities for personal training, spiritual growth and facilitating live events.

❑ I'd like to know how my church or group can use *FaithSearch* training and outreach resources, or can schedule a live event. Please call or send information.

Name:_____

Address:_____

City:_____ State/Province:_____

ZIP/Postal Code:_____ Country:_____

Phone:_____ E-mail:_____

Age Group: ❑ 12 & under ❑ Jr. High ❑ Sr. High ❑ 19-39 ❑ 40-59 ❑ 60+

FaithSearch
105 Peavey Rd., Ste 200
Chaska, MN 55318-2323
United States of America